TAKING THE MICKY

Being Micky Zany by Michael Lander

Michael Lander

To Sue & Ray
Love & Laughter

TAKING THE MICKY
(Being Micky Zany by Michael Lander)
Copyright ©2015 by Michael Lander

Published by
Mansion House Publishing
14 - 20 Wharfedale Road, Ipswich, Suffolk IP1 4JP

ISBN 978-0-9932587-0-1

Printed in ENGLAND
by ColourplanPrint
14 - 20 Wharfedale Road, Ipswich, Suffolk IP1 4JP

Dedication

This book will be a legacy for my children and their children. It goes out to my Lesley, friends and family who have helped me throughout my life and have given me the confidence to go on stage; and to my mum and dad who gave me all the love a son could ever want.

This story is dedicated to all those who have believed in me.

Contents

Chapter		Page

Foreword

In May 2005 Micky celebrated twenty-five years in show business and thought it would be a good idea to put pen to paper and tell his story so far. A tale about a quiet, unassuming, shy Suffolk lad who made a career out of making people laugh. However, it seems to have taken forever to write this forthcoming best seller as it is now early 2015!

He sees it as a sort of legacy for his children and grandchildren to read to get some sort of insight into his life, his thinking, and his time treading the boards. Mind you, a lot has happened over this last ten years or more, so taking the time to complete this masterpiece has been well worth the wait!

His early thoughts were how many people would be interested in reading about his life and his thoughts on comedy. A lack of confidence was already beginning to show. The book takes in his lifetime experiences to date, unlike some, who have written their memoirs when barely out of nappies.

He has performed for over thirty-five years to hundreds and thousands of people, millions in some cases when taking in his TV appearances. He is optimistic that many people will enjoy reading about his life, the first half a regular guy with no reference to bowel movements or stage fright, and the second half a successful 'almost famous' comedy entertainer.

Micky has a saying; 'those that matter......matter'.

This might be a night out for you.....it's a career for me.

He has had an eventful life with lots of ups and downs, and happily more ups than downs, but he never, ever thought it possible that he could become a professional comedian. In 1978 he realised this could happen after the seed was sown two years earlier. Even today after all these years as a funny guy there are some who are still very sceptical and do not think of comedy as a profession. A comedian, a proper job.....don't make me laugh!

"When I told people I was going to be a comedian, they all laughed. Well, they're not laughing now!"   *(Thank you Mr Monkhouse)*

There have been highs and lows along the way, but he has never looked back and wished he was doing something else. Micky has no regrets about that.

Most people will tell you that a comic has the hardest job in show business. If it is not the hardest, it can certainly be the loneliest.

He has always been a shy person; some might find that hard to believe but he now realises that comedy is what he was born to do. His vocation in life, his passion.

Some people might ask, is it an alter ego? He says it must be. Shyness can be a form of arrogance, but a nice arrogance and with comedy there can also be a dark side that sometimes needs to be addressed.

I might be schizophrenic, I don't know. I'm in two minds!

What better way to overcome this shyness than to stand in front of an audience and make them cry with laughter. There must be something deep rooted inside that makes him want to do this – masochism comes to mind!

Being funny, trying to compete with the very best and trying to reach the top of this profession is a serious business. There has been and always will be lots of competition which is essential in any walk of life. Being naturally funny certainly helps and Micky couldn't have pursued a career in comedy if he didn't feel funny!

Micky found out early on that to succeed in the comedy jungle you must have your own unique flair and be able to revamp, re-cycle and freshen up old material and ideas, or better still, write your own material! Observation and true to life situations are the key in this funny world we live in!

Comedy has changed so much over the years especially on TV. It is now increasingly important to put together your own style and original content to achieve a very high standard of performance and compete with the best.

In the eighties there were working men's clubs, social clubs, cabaret and night clubs, holiday camps, theatres, summer seasons, stag and hen nights, pubs and so forth and they were rife with entertainment. As we moved into the nineties and beyond, there has been a decline in these venues. Hopefully today, we may begin to see a return to more variety and live entertainment.

Nowadays, the more successful and busier comedians will be working the likes of the private functions, corporate events, cruising and the Comedy Store circuit in order to achieve quality of work. Success on TV today will undoubtedly come from those who have plied their trade in the comedy clubs and bars around the country which in contrast has now become the mainstream. Comedy is more prevalent today than ever, it is the new Rock 'n' Roll with the Edinburgh Fringe

Festival being a major event in the annual comedy calendar.

With many comedy clubs scattered around the UK now and the original new programmes on TV, comedy is well and truly more popular than ever with new generations. Micky finds almost all comedians funny with their different styles and material, including those from across the pond in the USA. He still loves what he does even more than ever and it is fair to say that he would want to be a comic if he had his time over again.

I've just joined the Reincarnation Society. It cost me five hundred pounds, you only live once don't ya!

It is not the air he breathes, it is not an addiction or obsession, it is a drug. Adrenalin is a wonderful thing!

It is not a job, far from it. Micky sees it as a passion, an art form and a craft. To go on to a stage and have an audience in the palm of your hand and watch them laughing, sometimes uncontrollably, it is a truly wonderful feeling. It can be very nerve racking and even today he still gets incredibly nervous, the bigger the venue the worse it is, or better, whichever way you look at it. It is good to get these nerves but once he gets on stage Micky feels at home. Some people will say it's a gift and he has kept the receipt!

Micky feels blessed that he has been born with this gift.

Losing his parents was very traumatic for Micky, especially his beloved mum. It took them a while to adjust to his new career change (from civil engineer to comedian) but they loved what he did and were so proud of 'their boy'.

Micky has now been married and divorced three times but he has no regrets, well not many! He still hopes to find love, romance, his soul mate and everlasting happiness with that special one to grow old with. Since completing this 'work of art' his personal life has made a significant change for the better and fate has dealt him a winning hand. Read on to find out more........

This book tells us how a shy boy from the back waters of Suffolk had not the slightest inkling of being in show business but fell into it by pure chance, or it was just meant to be, as he likes to think. There is no history of anyone in his family treading the boards but deep down early on there must have been this burning desire to get on stage and make a fool of himself. As already mentioned, he has performed to millions, but he has not yet sustained enough high profile to be a household name in the public eye. Whether he has not been in the right place at the right time or been seen by the right people........who knows?

Micky would love to taste the sweet smell of success that TV brings today and therefore gain wider acknowledgement and respect.

It must be wonderful to get a standing ovation when you walk onto a stage and it is a great feeling to get one when you walk off as well!

He is a somewhat nervous, insecure country boy, lacking in self-confidence and striving constantly to improve his technique and craft. Micky is constantly trying to find new ideas and material and, more importantly, to be that little bit different from all the others. As a comedian he feels that you have to be clever, do your homework and most importantly be yourself.

This book is about the life of a comedian who came from a humble, but very happy background and an insight into what it has been like to make people laugh professionally for all these years. It is an honest and nostalgic look into the career of a well-respected funny boy, a working comic who has yet to get that big break.

Micky wants this hard-hitting and gritty book to be made into a film! You can tell our boy's a bit of a dreamer – but a funny one!

He still dreams on, not necessarily to find any hint of fame, but to keep the passion and maintain the enthusiasm and inventiveness to write his own material and enjoy doing what he does best.

I'm not even a household name in my own home!

Micky will dream on. If we don't have dreams we have nothing. When you are on stage you become exactly who you are meant to be. Your true potential is only limited by your own imagination and determination. Therefore there is no limit to what you can achieve!

This is his story............

Chapter One

Cometh the Hour, Cometh the Funny Man

On a cold, wet winter's morning, Michael Dennis Lander, son of Dennis Frederick and Barbara Daphne, came into the World making his first public appearance. I was born at a very early age just outside of wedlock!.... on the 30th of November, St. Andrew's day. I spent my first few days in hospital because I wanted to be with my mum!

My mum and dad only had two children. They read that every third child born in the World was Chinese!

I wasn't a pretty baby. When I was born I was so ugly they smacked my mum!

I was late being born, probably my first signs of shyness, but when I appeared I had a big smile on my face or so they thought. They then realised I was upside down!

My mother was in labour so long they had to shave her twice!

Seriously, I was born with a smile on my face, I must have slept funny in the womb! That shining light in the delivery room was probably a spotlight for me to make my stage debut.....what an entrance!

When I was born King George VI was on the throne, Yul Brynner was the King in The King and I, Nat King Cole was number one with Mona Lisa and Elvis was about to be the King of Rock 'n'Roll. Then amongst all these Kings, a Joker was born!

It was the year that The Goon Show was first broadcast and the Archers first aired on the BBC Light Programme on radio. Also, films were given an X-rated certificate, Zebra crossings appeared on our roads and the Miss World Beauty Contest began.

The Peak District became Britain's first National Park, Newcastle won the FA Cup beating Blackpool 2-0, and Churchill won the General Election at the grand old age of seventy-six!

My parents wanted to name me after my father. I'm glad they didn't, it would have been silly to call me 'Dad!'

After ten weeks they had me circumcised. Sore? I couldn't walk for twelve months!

I was a cheeky, naughty, mischievous little boy. Until I was seven I thought my name was 'Shut Up!'

We had a naughty step in my house and mine was on the roof!

I was an unwanted child. When I was little my dad would throw me in the air…. and walk away!

They took me to an orphanage and said, mingle!

We played hide and seek once and I managed to find them two years later!

My mum went for a termination. They said it's too late once he's started school!

She got morning sickness…. AFTER I was born!

I have always lived in Suffolk…….mainly for tax reasons! Mum and dad had a council flat on the Maidenhall Estate in Ipswich, just a stone's throw from the town centre; so close in fact, that all our windows were broken!

Maidenhall wasn't the most salubrious part of Ipswich but it was by no means the roughest. You will always find one or two dodgy areas in every town and city where the residents are;

Always helping the Police with their enquiries!

Every garden has a fridge and a mattress!

The dustmen deliver!

11

And even the Wheelie bin is on four bricks!

I had a very good upbringing, my parents set good standards and we knew how far to go before we had a clip round the ear and were sent to bed early.

My dad was like a father to me!

He only hit me once when I was a child. He was driving a Ford Cortina at the time!

We had a quicksand at the bottom of our garden, I was an only child... eventually!

My parents never divorced – neither wanted custody!

For my sixth birthday all I got was a jigsaw... it nearly took my arm off!

When I was seven they bought me a radio and a toaster and said they were bath toys!

Mum worked at the local Churchman's Cigarette Factory, everybody seemed to work there and the building still remains after all these years. Dad was a Plasterer, the hardest job in the building trade. He worked hard and there was plenty of work about at the time. My father was by no means an intellectual, he disagreed and once said that he had an HQ of 150! I would labour for him for a while in my teens to earn some money before leaving school. Manual labour was too much like hard work and not for me I thought.

My shyness and lack of confidence, especially in those early years, definitely came from my dad. He was no leader and would stay in the background most of the time. He said very little, but when he did, it could be light hearted and quite humorous. He had a great sense of humour, thank God for that!

My dad loved to sing, he had a good voice but would need to be almost dragged up onto the stage at our local Trades and Labour Club in the town centre to give everybody a rendition of his favourite songs. My sister and I never saw this hidden talent as we had to sit in the back of the Ford Anglia with our fizzy Vimto drink and Oxo flavoured crisps...I do miss those Oxo flavoured crisps!

We could hear the rapturous applause that dad would receive and a free pint to boot! He would take their wild reaction almost apologetically…..I wonder who I take after!

This is probably the only show business blood in the family, my dad singing for his supper in the local Working Mens Social Club back in the fifties.

Everything seemed so much slower back then, not the technology that we have today. Simple, happy days!

I remember my childhood with great fondness. Before the Ford Anglia came along we had a Combination, a motorbike with a sidecar attached. All four of us on route to the seaside, mum and dad with their helmets and goggles on, looking like extras from The Great Escape! Then there was the two of us sticking our heads out of the plastic covered roof of the sidecar holding on for dear life and singing; 'She'll be coming round the mountain when she comes! She'll be coming round the mountain…'

I remember dad playing his 78 rpm records on our first record player, a blue and white Dansette. The Inkspots, The Platters, Johnny Ray, Guy Mitchell, Kay Starr, Doris Day, Alma Cogan…… all legends!

My dad remained a plasterer until he called it a day after turning fifty, a tough occupation working mainly in damp, empty houses which were just a shell. It was very cold in those winter months, back when winters were winters! He had a trial with Ipswich Town Football Club; they found him guilty! He could have gone further with his football aspirations or so he said. To be honest I do not think he had the desire, the passion or determination. He jokingly blamed being with my mum, but I think it was a lack of ambition. That is where we differed.

My granddad, on my dad's side, was a professional Boxer. He fought in the ring well into his fifties, an amazing feat, and even came up against the legendary Freddie Mills! George, my granddad, had all the attributes of a fighter in those days, a punched in nose and a cauliflower ear, he had the full set!

My dad also boxed in the Army so it seemed natural to them to give young Micky boy a set of boxing gloves for his seventh birthday. Fighting was just not in my blood I'm glad to say and it could never be my game or sport. I had a few rounds and even a few fights, I gave it a good try but decided early on in my career that it wasn't for me. I retired early….I was eight!

I had so many knock downs I ended up with a cauliflower arse!

Then I saw this face in the crowd that I recognized. It was mine!

I fought this one guy and I had him scared, he thought he'd killed me!

I did hurt him though. He slipped in my blood!

I had to retire early, I got stomach problems…no guts!

You certainly need to be clever and have a fighting instinct to be a comic but Boxing, no thanks! Fighting for laughs would turn out to be a lot less painful, well, most of the time!

Chapter Two

School Days – The Class Clown

As you can imagine, technology was a million light years away from where we are today. A black and white telly, only two channels, starting at 4.30 pm in the afternoon and finishing before 11.00pm at night. As a very young lad I can remember conkers, marbles, tiddlywinks, Yo-yos and skipping ropes and many other simple games to play and then when girls came along I thought, sod these for a laugh!

We had cops and robbers, cowboys and indians, doctors and nurses. Unlucky bugger me. I was always the Ambulance Driver!

I went to Luther Road Primary School on the Maidenhall Estate, I was five years old. There was no pre-school, nursery or school-runs in those days. No mums picking up their kids from school in their four-by-four BMW tractors. We had to walk home in all weathers! I liked school as far as I can remember and now I try to see the funny side of life including those school days and growing up.

My three worst subjects at school were maths and arithmetic!

We never had an I-phone, I-pad, I-pod in my day. We had; I think, I read, I write!

We never had e-mails, we had telegrams and we wrote letters. No computers, we had Etch-a-Sketch! We didn't download, e-mail, Facebook or Google. We didn't surf the net, Wi-Fi, Txt or Tweet. We never had mobile phones; walkie talkies were all the fashion and if your mum and dad couldn't afford them we had two tin cans and a piece of string!

Back in those days crack was a laugh, smack was painful and a joint was a Sunday dinner!

We never had Rap, Hip Hop or Garage music. We never had a frigging garage!

We used to get spanked by a middle aged woman – you would pay a lot of money for that today!

What do you want to be when you grow up son? I wanna go into property dad. I wanna be a burglar!

I passed my eleven plus...when I was eighteen! (joke). It was the sixties and I had got through my first decade without being bullied. I used to carry the boxing gloves everywhere! I went to Northgate Grammar School for Boys, only minutes from where we lived. Mum was overjoyed but I wasn't. All my buddies had gone to the Secondary Modern School –where they played football. I was stuck with rugby, hockey and tennis – no football and no girls!

I hated it to start with but it did get better. I loved football with a passion and still do. My father was a decent right winger and I took after him, we both had the same size shorts! As I moved into my teens, sounds like a good direction to go, I was playing for several local teams. I later played for the Great Eastern Hotel, a Sunday morning pub team, and then another local pub, the Eastern Union Railway team. These were two very good sides and we won many medals and cups. On Saturday afternoons I played for Achilles and Westerfield which were both also very good teams in the premier division of the local league. I wasn't the best by any means, spending more time in the respective Reserve teams but every now and again I would be promoted to the First Team and I had my moments!

I still support my home team, Ipswich Town, and I used to go and watch them play many times in the early days of the Alf Ramsey era. With Alf at the helm we won the 1961/1962 League Title and it was the start of some great years ahead for the 'Tractor Boys' culminating in FA Cup success in 1978 and then winning the UEFA Cup in 1981. Sir Alf, as he later became, used to play golf at my local club in Rushmere where I still play today. Long after winning the World Cup with England he would regularly be in a four ball in front of us on Thursday mornings for many years. He was a lovely man, quiet and unassuming, we never talked tactics but he was a true gentleman and is still revered at the Golf Club today.

My interest in comedy goes back to my early teens. I used to collect a weekly comedy magazine entitled Comedy Half Hour containing jokes and sketches. I would write down the jokes that I liked and thought were funny and then start to assemble my own gag book, not knowing I would one day be telling jokes for a living, some of this material I would rely on when I started.

Looking back, even in those days there must have been something deep inside me but I was yet to know that comedy would play a major part in the years that lay ahead.

As a schoolboy I would be the class clown. Not in a loud, arrogant way but in a quiet, unassuming way. I had an impish cheek – the other one was ok! School was good, I wasn't the brightest or cleverest guy in the class but I had a decent memory and this would help when it came to revising. Also, this would go on to help me in the future when remembering and telling jokes but in those early days not being able to talk 'proper' was a problem to say the least.

I had an unfortunate.......s s s s stammer!

Chapter Three

Puppy Love

Apart from my shyness and being somewhat introvert I also had a very unfortunate stammer.

To be frank, no, not a name change, with being so shy and having a slight peech insediment, sorry, speech impediment, it's hard to believe that I became a stand-up comedian! People would ask, is it a problem having a stammer, and I would say no, it comes easy to me!

I said to the fellow beside me in the hospital bed, "w.w.w.what you in for?" He replied, "prostate gland." I said, "w.w.w.what's that?" He said, "I used to piddle like you talk!"

One time in school, it was my turn to speak in front of the whole Assembly. I couldn't face the embarrassment and bunked off school, feigning illness. How sad is that?!

Can you imagine today, not liking an audience, turning back and going home? Mind you, there have been many times when I've arrived at certain gigs and wanted to do a runner!

That would have been the easy way out. You learn from the bad ones they say. Many times I've asked myself what am I doing here?! However, being able to make the girls laugh has always been an advantage. I think most ladies would put a sense of humour on the top of their list.

Shyness wasn't such a bad thing but having a stammer, I c.c.can't be s.s.sure about t.t.that!

I went twelve years without sex... then when I was 13!

I shan't forget my first time. I was really scared....I was on my own!

I said, "Are you a virgin?" She said, "No, not yet."

I asked this girl, "Is this your first time?" She said, "With you it is!"

I thought I was really turning her on, then she told me she had asthma!

She was wearing those fishnet tights, when she took them off, her bum looked like a waffle!

Dawn was my very first girlfriend, yes I know the gag, up at the crack of dawn! Then I met Sally, we seemed to break it off more often than not, (oooh), but it all was good experience for growing up in those innocent teenage years.

I realised early on that when I was out with friends telling funny gags and stories and doing the odd impression, it would give me comfort and confidence and help me overcome the shyness and awkwardness. I loved it when people laughed, it was a buzz even at that time. I became the centre of attention albeit for a few minutes or so and just maybe my friends, girls especially, would get to like me because I made them laugh. I was not the best chatter upper in the world! It was quite tough to start with:

"Can I have your phone number?" "Yes, it's in the book!" "Your name?!" "It's in the book as well!"

"I could make you very happy." "Why, are you leaving?!"

"How come you're so beautiful?" "I must have got your share!"

"What sign were you born under?" "Do not enter!"

"Can I have this dance?" "Yeah, I don't want it!"

Girls can be so bitchy!

I used to get my own back. Not all the girls were that good looking, they would say:

"I'm looking forward to my beauty sleep". I thought, I don't think so!

We had a beauty contest once; sponsored by Oil of Ugly! Nobody won!!

This one girl boasted:

Beauty runs in my family. I thought, it must have galloped past you!

Beauty is only skin deep. She must have been born inside out!

She was so bandy, if she wore black tights and red knickers, she looked like a magnet!

She had everything a man could wish for... a beard, moustache, muscles.

It was so embarrassing to go into a chemist back in those days and ask for.... condominiums.......conundrums.....condoms! There would be a young girl serving and I'd end up asking for a toothbrush!

I would take the girls behind the bushes.....and clean their teeth!

"Can I have a packet of condoms please?" She asked, "Large or small?" I said, "Large of course!" She gave me a box of fifty!

I left Grammar School with nine O'levels. Yes, nine O'levels! Having a good memory was the key – like today. I tried one term of A'levels but after much thought I decided another two years studying and possibly University was not for me. I had one or two part-time jobs before I left school; I was a paper boy when I was much younger, who wasn't? I only had to do two roads; the A12 and the A45 (joke)! When I was sixteen I had a fun time working Friday evenings and Saturdays at Sainsbury's in Ipswich town centre. Those were the days of no self-service and sawdust on the floor! I served at the poultry counter, I really enjoyed it, having a laugh. Even back in those early days I was always a cheeky bugger, "Leg or breast madam?!" The women loved a bit of sauce with their chicken!

A lady walks in, grabs a chicken, shoves it up her jumper and starts to leave the shop. The butcher says, "What are you doing with that?" The lady replied, "Peas, carrots and a few potatoes!"

I joined an Accountancy firm in Ipswich town centre. Since I had just acquired O'level Mathematics, mum and dad knew someone who could get me a job as an assistant clerk, checking figures all day, nine till five, five days a week. I stuck it for six months. I don't know what was more boring, Accountancy or death!

A Doctor said to a lady patient, "You only have six months to live." She said, "oh no, what shall I do?" The doctor replied, "If I were you I would marry an Accountant." She said, "Will I live longer?" "No, it will just seem like it!"

For my Accountant's birthday present I got him some receipts. I said if you don't like them, I've kept the presents!

I still rely on my wealth of accountancy experience today and use it in my act now, especially at corporate functions, hoping for an Accountant to be in the audience. My very good friend John McNally happens to be my Accountant but also a golf buddy and we socialise regularly. He is great with figures, especially his wonderful wife Andrea! We have also cruised together on occasions. They have a great sense of humour, thank goodness for that!

An Accountant emailed his wife:
You are now fifty-four years old and I have certain needs which you are no longer able to satisfy. I am otherwise happy with you as a wife and I hope you will not be hurt or offended to learn that I am at the Grand Hotel with my eighteen year old secretary and I will be home very late.
An hour later he receives an email back:
You too are fifty-four years old and by the time you get this I will be at the Hilton Hotel with our eighteen year old gardener. I know you are a first class Accountant so you can easily work out that eighteen goes into fifty-four more than fifty-four goes into eighteen. Don't wait up!

After the excitement of the Accounts Department and through more friends of mum and dad, I went into Civil Engineering. I have O'levels in Art, Surveying and Technical Drawing, fancy that!

I worked for Jackson Group of Kesgrave, Ipswich, obtaining an ONC and HNC in Civil Engineering at the local Suffolk College. I did enjoy this work a lot better, setting out and surveying, with a lot of outdoor work to boot.

When the point of no return arrived and my proper job was to come to an end I would have no regrets. My mind would be on other things and a big decision would have to be made, but that was not to happen for another ten years!

I met a girl called Pauline who would turn out to be my first serious relationship. It was a blind date and her brother set me up, sorry…set us up! He also happened to be courting my sister Jan at the time and they themselves have now been married for over forty years.

I had so many blind dates when I was young they gave me a free dog!

We met at the Manor Ballroom in Ipswich. The venue is still around today as a function room and is also the Jokers Comedy Club, a thriving comedy event once a month. The stammer was still there, more so when I was nervous. On our first date Pauline asked for a Britvic orange. B's were a particular problem for me and still are today, so she ended up with a Gin and Tonic! Consequently, she thought I was trying to get her drunk – as if! I blamed the Barman!

We would go out with friends and I would secretly have a few gags up my sleeve, like a true pro! Just in case the moment came and I was asked to lighten the mood I would be ready! Preparation is everything – fail to prepare, prepare to fail!

One of our regular haunts in those latter teenage years was the Copford Windmill near Colchester. Many comedians would appear at this venue, two on both Fridays and Saturdays, the more well-known ones being Charlie Smithers, Jimmy Jones and Mike Reid. They were all brilliant, I was in awe watching these funny men saying funny lines with all the audience laughing and having a great night. It was my first taste of seeing live comedians, as I had only previously seen the laughter makers on television before.

It was quite a whirlwind romance with Pauline, we were engaged after a year and soon married at St. Augustine's Church in Ipswich on a sunny day in May.

I didn't have to get married….she did!

I shan't forget those four words I said to her when I proposed, "You're not are ya?!" (This didn't apply to Pauline I hasten to add!)

I remember her father saying to me, "Can you support a family?" I said, "Of course." He replied, "Good there are six of us!"

The in-laws were lovely people, very down to earth, lots of class......working class. At least my mother-in-law Jane could take a joke, which was a blessing.

She once said, "What's that horrible picture in the hallway?" I said, "It's a mirror!"

She used to wet the bed, so for her birthday I bought her an electric blanket!

"Shall we have my mother down for the weekend?" I replied, "She'll be OK in the loft!"

On the television at this time was the Johnny Hamp comedy show called The Comedians. It was over forty years ago and how standards have changed with regard to the material and what is acceptable or not. It is called being PC – welcome to PC World!

Comedy standards then were far less stringent, especially on TV. There was more racist, ageist and sexist material around then and looking back I am amazed they got away with it. Today, in an ever changing inclusive society, standards have improved dramatically which can only be for the better.

We lived in Bramford, a small village just outside of Ipswich, virtually in the countryside, very peaceful and very quiet. Looking back, life seemed to be a lot slower, but then came the moment when I first took to the stage, or should I say, was forced up on to the stage!

Chapter Four

The Comedy Seed

It was the long, hot summer of 1976 – isn't that a film title? I only wish this next piece was as sultry and moving as the film! In hindsight, this night was to set the seed for my introduction to the comedy world. We were with friends on holiday at Pontins Holiday Camp at Pakefield, near Lowestoft, not too far from where we lived on the East coast of Suffolk. Claire, our daughter, was waiting to be born in the October, she wasn't in a queue or anything, and Pauline had a massive bump, so she was not feeling her best which was made all the worse by this very hot August evening.

My cousin Steve was there and he was the instigator in getting me up on stage in the first place. I would never have had the nerve or confidence to do such a thing on my own but he became the catalyst for my career in comedy.

This reminds me of my dad being physically forced up on stage at our local Labour Club all those years ago. Pontins had a talent show contest that night which all the holiday centres had at the time. I'm sure they still do today but not on the same grand scale.

This was my introduction to show business, over thirty eight years ago, there were no videos and not even a photograph to remind me of what I looked like at the time. I had never been on a stage before or even held a microphone. At that time we thought that it would be a one off, a bit of a laugh, just some holiday fun. It was only an amateur talent show all said and done and the first prize was a week's holiday at Pakefield. The second prize was two weeks holiday!

No matter how bad it goes, the average holiday maker will always cheer and clap the amateur, usually! Steve and I had to quickly think of what we could do, we had never been in this position before. I was nervous, well wouldn't you be? Steve sang, he has a very good voice, and we did a few jokes. I did my Norman Wisdom impression, I could do him as soon as I was born! To close the act, I say act loosely, we performed our rendition of 'Whispering Grass'which had gone to number one in the charts in the previous year, with Windsor Davies and Don Estelle.

We had a rehearsal, thank goodness, and we were set to go. At the end of the day nothing was at stake except our pride and letting our family and friends

down. The last thing you want to do is make a fool of yourself, well I did but......
well you know what I mean! Here is some of the material we did.

I said to Steve, "What is that there?" He replied, "It's a birth mark." I said, "How long have you had that?"

I went to a nightclub last night wearing jump leads instead of a tie and the Bouncer said, "OK come in, but don't start anything."

I said to Steve, "My cat does his jobbies on the newspaper," He replied, "That's good isn't it?" I said, "No, I'm still reading it!"

"I took our dog to the vets because I'm having him put down." Steve said, "Why is that?" I said, "My arms are killing me!"

"I went to the Cemetery today." He asked, "Who's dead?" I said, "They all are!"

It took me six months to do a jigsaw. Not bad, it said three to five years on the box!

We came joint first out of twelve acts. Joint first! It was like winning Britain's Got Talent today, well nearly! We had a playoff with the other act, a female singer. She won the outright first prize –it turned out she was an ex-professional and what's more, her son was the drummer in the backing band. What a fix!

I have never trusted a talent show since, hark at me, it was only an amateur talent contest, just a bit of fun I hear you say. What fame can do for you!

We spent many a childhood holiday at Pakefield Holiday Camp in the sixties, there was no travelling, back packing, gap year or holidaying abroad then. No Algarve, Disney World or Costa Packet and there were certainly no cruises!

Since turning professional I have performed hundreds of shows at Pakefield regularly over the years. My good friend, Graham Henry, the Entertainments Manager there since 1966, left in 2011 and it will never be the same without him. He was Mr. Pakefield, bless you mate, I know one day we will meet again and I am quietly confident you will buy me that drink!

Chapter Five

Special Delivery – It's a Girl!

After our shock success in coming joint first at Pakefield, we waited for the phone to ring for offers. Nothing, not even a wrong number! I know it wasn't exactly The X Factor or winning a comedy award but to me it was the beginning. I didn't know then where it would lead to but I had got the bug and the seed was sown. It was only a few minutes on stage but I loved it and it felt good especially afterwards, but not before, as I was so nervous!

More importantly, there then came a very special delivery. Claire Louise was born weighing in at 7lb 6oz. I was so proud to be there, what a fantastic moment!

It was a natural birth, there was no blood, screaming or drugs......unlike the conception!

It was so long ago but I can remember the day so vividly. I had gone to work, the proper job that is, and as I was arriving on-site in Colchester, Essex, which was half an hour from home, one of the lads came out of the site office and shouted, "the water's broke". He had obviously just spoken to Pauline on the phone, but I stupidly thought that we had got a leak in one of the main drain pipes we had laid on-site the day before. I said, "Get the boys there quickly and let them have a look." He said, "It's your missus, HER water's broke, you daft bugger! Go back home now and take this mop with you!"

It was 9.30 am in the morning and Claire was born nine hours later at 6.50 pm, Crossroads was on the telly! What a day, a natural birth, no gas and air, I was absolutely fine! It was the 14th of October, that long hot summer of 1976 and the talent show now paled into insignificance. I was a dad – and a very proud one at that.

A year passed before Steve and I were to tread the boards for a second time. A year of watching Claire slowly changing from a beautiful baby into a gorgeous little girl.

Chapter Six

Split Personality

A small pub in Sudbury, Suffolk, was holding a Pub Entertainer of the Year Competition. So once again Steve thought it would be good for us to enter. We weren't exactly on a roll, it was over a year since our last success and we would need to put together a slightly different act, I say act loosely, we had only done one gig! I say gig loosely again as that lasted only seven minutes!

It wasn't the big ballroom with the large audience of Pontins and we didn't have the luxury of a four piece backing band like last time. Sudbury is a very nice laid back town in lazy Suffolk, tractor boy country, and the pub in question had a small lounge which was packed to the rafters with the locals and our supporters. The atmosphere was electric, yes Sudbury actually had electricity at the time, and the pub had never seen anything at all like this before and were in for a treat! To our surprise the accompaniment was two old boys, one with a grand piano and the other a double bass. We never thought for a second that this would be a problem, after all, what experience did we have, it was just another amateur night – what did we have to lose? I suppose thinking about it now, we must have been trying and hoping to do well, then maybe go on to perform other shows and earn some pin money to add to our weekly income. We gave the band our music, I say band and music very loosely! The song was You To Me Are Everything, a recent hit for the soul band The Real Thing.

My cousin and I were taking our second visit to the stage, albeit on a worn out carpet in a small country pub, about to attempt a soul number with a backing band consisting of only a grand piano and double bass! We gave them the sheet music and it was like giving my one year old daughter a Rubik Cube, remember them? I was in one key, Steve in another and the duo were in a third key, the full set! I can't tell you what it sounded like but I am sure you can imagine! We didn't have monitors or speakers to hear ourselves through and not much feedback from the audience either come to think of it! I still shudder when looking back all these years later. We didn't even a have a run through or rehearsal with the band beforehand!

I recall Steve asking someone in the audience, "Are we singing too near the microphone?" To which they replied, "You are singing too near the pub!" We only did a gag or two and a couple of impressions as well to get them on our side. After we crucified the song, the silence was deafening!

It was so bad we were boo'd off and then boo'd back on again!

Steve said to me that they hated us from the start and I replied sarcastically, "Well it saves time!"

A monk broke a twenty year vow of silence to heckle us!

Even now looking back, it is hard to describe how devastated we felt. I believe the term used in show business circles is called dying on your arse! Our friends and family, no they weren't a BT cheap phone rate, were all stood at the front and we had quite a lot of support there.

However, by the time we had murdered the song and finished the spot from Hell they were all backing out into the car park doubled up in hysterical laughter.

We had the crowd behind us but managed to lose them five miles later.

We came eighth in the competition and only seven took part! We got beaten by a spoon player and that's the truth. He was only taking them back to the kitchen and that's a gag! Our road to fame, or country lane more like it, had taken a knock or better still, a very loud bang. We never gave up, oh no, we were determined to carry on – won one, lost one, not bad!

We thought long and hard about a name for the double act. Someone suggested The Real Thing, we told them politely to go forth and multiply! We were not going to let the Sudbury debacle get us down so we decided to give talent shows a wide berth – for a while anyway. Stevie came up with Split Personality, a great name for a double act – so that was it. We had a name, two talent shows and we were ready to take on the entertainment world.

As you slide down the bannister of life make sure the splinters are facing the right way!

As my Granddad once said. If you go on that stage and only get just one laugh – you're rubbish!

It was amateur, no money changed hands. We were the best in our price range!

Chapter Seven

Going Solo

Not much happened for a while, we thought the whole world had heard about the Sudbury experience! We shouldn't have had to take all the blame, it wasn't our fault the band couldn't read music. They should have told us – muppets!

Anyway, it wasn't rocket science, we had our proper jobs, our families and maybe the thought of being the next Morecambe and Wise, Mike and Bernie Winters, Batman and Robin or Cameron and Clegg was just a pipe dream!

1978 came and the year started on a big high for our double act at least. Split Personality were to be the star attraction at the Manor Ballroom, Ipswich, where I had met Pauline on our first date. In those days it was a fabulous venue, we had Bluesville on a Monday night with Nanda and Ron Lesley from the USA who played all the latest sounds from America. It was a really hip place to be in the late sixties and seventies.

The football teams that I played for at the time had an end of season dinner dance and presentation evening and suggested that it would be ideal for us to perform at the event. The nightmare of Sudbury six months earlier, had obviously not reached their social secretaries. This memory was never going to leave us but we had learnt hard and fast and had put together a much better set. The gig went very well and we were gaining experience and what's more, there wasn't a grand piano or double bass in sight!

We didn't get paid for this performance so that might have had something to do with our success! Money talks, but not in this case! We were back and so was our confidence, but for how long?

At the Football presentation event we were accompanied superbly by a backing duo, Vision Two, George and Terry, two good friends of ours. We performed at one or two more clubs with the boys, Westgate Ward Club and Gainsborough Labour Club, both in Ipswich, the latter was to be my first solo performance as a professional. At another local gig we performed with the Mayfair Trio, an elderly band who had been around locally for years. The drummer was somewhat deaf so the organist had to tap him with his hand on the top of his head when counting in at the start of each song! I laugh now just thinking about it.

All seemed to be picking up nicely and then came a really tough gig just on the outskirts of Ipswich at The Limes Hotel at Needham Market. They were pig farmers and a pig of an audience too! The band could not read music and to make things worse when they played our introduction, yours truly was on the loo! Twenty minutes later after ploughing our way through the noisy bunch of pig farmers I left the stage to go back to the loo. It may have been the smell of the pigs! I remember coming back and whispering in Steve's ear, "I've started the car!" We would open up the act with the ever popular song Proud Mary, then a Drifters medley and Steve would then attempt a Gladys Night hit while I tried to put him off with some visuals; impressions of Frank Spencer, John Wayne, Dame Edna and a funny Kung Fu sketch, remember grasshopper? There would be a gaggle of gags, then we would close the act with the song Tie a Yellow Ribbon. We always had Whispering Grass in reserve! Not bad for an amateur duo with no experience, if I say so myself.

A few weeks later the Maltings Nightclub in Stowmarket, yet another small Suffolk town, were to hold a New Faces style talent show, yes another one, but this was on a much grander scale. New Faces had been running on ITV for a couple of years or so and it was a very popular TV talent show format. The BBC had Opportunity Knocks hosted by Hughie Green, remember back then there were only two channels. New Faces attracted millions of viewers, I remember two years earlier such funny men as Jim Davidson and Lenny Henry becoming household names. Ironically, yours truly was to be on the actual TV show a few years later. However, I am ahead of myself and on the 7th of March Split Personality entered heat four in that Stowmarket Maltings talent show.

We only had limited material to use from our previous amateur gigs and hoped that this would get us through the heat. The judges included; BBC TV presenter David Clayton, Norwich Artistes Agent Brian Russell and Radio Orwell's Anthea Clarke. They said that we had potential, but did not gel too well as a duo and the chemistry wasn't quite there between us.

Steve was, and still is, a very good vocalist and went on to sing locally for many years and I was the funny one. We had not had much time to bond as a double act and gain experience which meant we hadn't quite got the chemistry right yet. Anyway, we didn't get through to the final.

A couple of weeks later after our disappointment, Steve entered the contest on his own and did very well but unfortunately he did not progress to the final.

The lads and I used to go every week to the heats as it was a good night out and very entertaining watching all the various acts do their bit. When Steve didn't get through he and the lads urged me to get up and tell some jokes. No way, Pedro! Me on my own up there, are you raving mad? It was ok in a double act when there were two of us and less pressure but with no Steve to guide me, no confidence, no bottle, and more importantly….no bloody act!!

What have you got to lose the lads said, just tell a few gags. There could have been one or two drinks involved and in the end I got up on stage feeling extremely nervous. So there I was entering this small town talent contest which was my first solo performance and I won the heat! I was in the final and it is hard to remember exactly what I did, but it went something like this:

I was out shopping today and I went into a pet shop. I said to the guy, "I want to buy a bumble bee." He replied, "We don't sell bumble bees." I said, "There's one in the window!"

I said to the man in the DIY store, "Can I have some 4 by 2 wood please?" He replied, "We're metric now, it's 100 by 50." I said, "How much?" He went, "Three pound a foot!"

"I want some nails." He asked, "How long do you want them?" I said, "I wanna keep them!"

"Can I have some rat poison please?" He said, "I will make some up for you; do you want to wait?" I said, "No, I'll send a rat round for it!"
He said, "Have you tried filling their holes with Polyfilla?" I said, "I can't catch em!"

I said to the Green Grocer, "Can I have a hundredweight of potatoes?" He said, "They're kilos now." I said, "Ok, can I have a hundredweight of kilos."

A 'not too bright' young man walks into a Builders Merchants and asks for thirteen thousand bricks. The fella behind the counter said, "That's a lot of bricks Sir?" He replied, "Yeah, I'm building a Barbecue." "That's a lot of bricks for a barbecue?" "Yeah, I'm on the tenth floor!"

I added impressions of Frank Spencer and Norman Wisdom and that was more or less what I did that night nearly thirty-seven years ago. Simple, clean gags, but the audience enjoyed what I did!

I must have felt excited and elated I'm sure, but then I still had no intention or idea where it was all going to lead. If it wasn't for Steve and the lads I would never have entered under my own steam, similar to my dad at the Labour Club I suppose. Shy Micky Lander had got the bug, and this was to be the very start and reason that I turned to comedy as a career. It was to be the end of the double act though, short but sweet. Split Personality had split and we had no regrets. Steve had given me that initial confidence and impetus to get up on stage in the first place and I have never forgotten that. We spent quite a lot of time together in those early years, fun times, he was always upbeat. I only wish we could see more of each other today and I will definitely try and make that happen.

The Final was a special night in more ways than one as Ipswich Town lifted the FA Cup that very same day beating Arsenal at Wembley and the winning goal was scored by local hero, Roger Osborne. The great Bobby Robson era was taking off and three years later we went on to win the UEFA Cup.

Sir Bobby Robson was a great man and a gentleman just like Sir Alf Ramsey. I cannot remember too much about the final, the Talent Show final that is, but I did well and came third. I couldn't believe it, a very special moment! I didn't have an act for goodness sake and no gigs under my belt but now after a handful of gags I was on cloud nine! I only entered for a laugh, that's a daft thing to say, of course I entered for a laugh!

Again the material was very simple and some of it was sourced from my Joke Book which I had been adding to over the years. What a Pro…well nearly!

Even from those early recollections I knew I wanted to keep the gags as short as possible. I didn't want to do any drawn out material as I only had a few minutes and I wanted to try and get in as many laughs as I could! Bang, Bang, Bang!

Also, I wanted to personalise the gags and revolve them around me, therefore making them more believable.

I like to perform observational humour through true to life situations which people can identify with. Sometimes, we need to laugh when we are confronted by stress and adversity surely?

Drink killed my Granddad; he got hit by a Guinness truck!

Drink and women killed my other Granddad, he couldn't get either so he shot himself!

I was celebrating my other Granddad's 103rd birthday last week. He wasn't there obviously!

When I was a little lad my Dad said to me, "We need to talk about the birds and the bees." I replied, "Well what do you wanna know then Dad?"

When I was young my mate said to me, "I know how babies are made." I replied, "I know how they're not!"

I said to him I found a contraceptive behind the radiator and he said, "What's a radiator?"

Just before I took to the stage that night, a group of Ipswich Town football supporters came into the club and they were in very good spirits, celebrating our historic win. We had just won the FA Cup and there was I, the local boy, in the final of a prestigious talent show....what could be better! The outright winners on the night were a professional pop band called Clown. They were very good so coming third to a professional group made me feel even more chuffed. If it had all stopped there I wonder how my life would have panned out? I had a wonderful family and a good profession but no inkling whatsoever of venturing into the comedy world. All I had done in the last twenty months was a local football freebie, a handful of local clubs and four talent shows, albeit only two on my own, just ten minutes or so of jokes and a few impressions to boot. Mind you, looking back, I suppose Steve and I thought it would be very satisfying just getting up there to entertain no matter what the outcome or consequence. We did it, and now I had done it, but up until now it was just fun. I mean winning talent shows is one thing but could I really make a living out of comedy? That was the real challenge.........

Chapter Eight

Zany by Name, Zany by Nature!

Clown were managed by Jonathan Clown aka John Walker. John must have seen something in me that night at the talent show and from then on took me under his wing. Through his own experiences working with the band and having certain contacts within the industry he assured me that he could get me work. Work, comedy, money, semi-professional status, it looked like I was on my way. John was a loveable jack the lad sort of character, quite flamboyant and he definitely had the gift of the gab!

He could sell the Pope a double bed!

John could certainly talk the talk, but the big question was, could he walk the walk! I liked John, it was hard not to. I wonder where he is now. If Clown had not been on the bill that night I wonder what would have happened. There we go again....fate. I believe in fate, even more so today.....LOL!

John was a great motivator, he promised me so much and inspired confidence in me. It was John who came up with the stage name 'Micky Zany'. He had made lots of contacts and assured me that work was plentiful as long as I was willing to travel. I had to remind him on many occasions though, that I had a very happy marriage, a young daughter, a steady job, qualifications, a pension, a Company car.... blah, blah, blah!

A few weeks after the Maltings Nightclub final I did another talent show. I know, not another one! Once again I had no intention of getting up on stage, I was on holiday with my family at Seacroft, a Pontins holiday centre at Hemsby, near Great Yarmouth. As it was at Pakefield two years earlier, they were having their weekly summer heats. Low and behold and as luck would have it, I won the heat.

I asked the girl in the Chemist for a bar of soap. She said, "Scented?" I said, "No, I'll take it now!"

I said to the girl in the Café, "Can you put four teas in this flask please, two with sugar!"

I told the Optician, "My eyes are bad." He replied, "They are, you're in the Fish and Chip Shop!"

"Cod and chips twice please." He replied, "I heard you the first time!"

Maybe I could make a career out of doing talent shows after all! I had done quite a few now and it was almost becoming second nature to me. Experience is everything, ha ha. There was just one thing missing, no money was exchanging hands being an amateur and all that.

I had nothing to compare these nights with, no one was paying to see me and there was no real pressure to perform, but I suppose without really knowing it I was gaining confidence in what I was trying to achieve. Delivery, timing and strong material were important to me even at this very early stage. The incentive of winning this heat at Seacroft was the Final in Blackpool......ta dah! I was starting to get a little bit more risqué with my material and talking about being married, women, family and so forth, spicing it up a little.

Innuendo.........isn't that an Italian suppository?!

Son and father in the bath together. The son said, "Dad, what's that thing down there?" Dad said, "It's my Rocket." To which the son replied, "It's a bit little for a Rocket." The Dad remarked, "It gets bigger as it gets closer to Ma's"

She smacked her husband for being a lousy lover. He smacked her back for knowing the difference!

The husband stands there with nothing on and asks his wife, "Do you notice anything different?" The wife replies, "No, nothing I haven't seen before." The husband replies, "It's pointing to my new shoes." To which she replied, "You should have bought a new hat!"

She said, "I have a severe hangover." He said, "Put your bra back on!"

He said, "I like black underwear." So she didn't wash her undies for a month!

You have to remember that this was the late seventies and I was just starting out as a Comedian. Much of this content now seems so dated and clubby, just mainly gags and one liners. I would later keep adding different material therefore unconsciously starting to build up my own small repertoire. There was no real need to change but I felt that it would make me feel fresh and I was now starting to throw in some impressions as well to beef up the act. What act you are asking? I was only doing five or ten minute slots! These impressions and impersonations would ultimately give the performance a lift.

The weeks were ticking by since that Cup Final day and John was keen to get me out there into the big wide world earning some money and gaining valuable experience. Also, the commission he would be receiving would come in handy for him! Most importantly we had to find out if I could cut the grade out there on the professional circuit. We all know in every walk of life experience counts for everything and it can take a very long time to build a successful act, one that is your own. Anyone today coming into the Comedy world doesn't necessarily need a wealth of material and experience, not to start with anyway. The climate has changed a lot since those days of the seventies and eighties where variety was rife. There was still lots of competition and I found out hard and fast that it wasn't going to happen overnight – far from it!

At first John sent me to some venues that I would never go to today. They were hard, tough and uncompromising places but we both felt that I had to experience these to toughen me up. These were the sort of places that I would have sent my mother-in-laws to….and left them there!

The mother-in-law said, "If I was married to you, I would put poison in your dinner." I replied, "If I was married to you, I'd bloody well take it!"

The Blackpool final was very rewarding. All the winners from each week of the season from all of the holiday parks were performing. The final was held at Pontins in Blackpool and hundreds of people auditioned, a bit like Britain's Got Talent today. Amazingly, I made the final twelve and came third…….again!

I was absolutely gob smacked and I still hadn't done a proper gig really! Some of the material was very raw and well used, but hey, you had to start somewhere. It was very early days back then!

We had our honeymoon in Blackpool – it's the one night in a man's life when he's in bed first!

I said, "What's the fur around the bottom of your nightie for?" She replied, "To keep my neck warm!"

She put her hand down my pyjama trousers and said, "What are these for?" I said, "Four?!"

I said, "I'll use the rhythm method." She replied, "Where will you find a guitar at 3 in the morning?!"

The morning after the honeymoon night she pulled the covers back and looked at my naked body. She said, "Is that all you've got left?!"

The late, great, Liverpool legend Emlyn Hughes presented me with my Trophy. I still have it today, it was like winning the FA Cup! We had our photograph taken together and I still have that as well. I treasure them both.

Like I have said, I never actually had an act as such but had just won through from hundreds of wannabes to come in the top three. I was over the moon, as Crazy Horse (Emlyn Hughes' nickname) would have said!

Chapter Nine

Show Me the Money

It wasn't long now before my first proper gig. I was a professional, sorry, semi-professional. The fee, a whopping great £15, less commission! The amount of the fee did not matter to me, getting paid for making people laugh felt so good. It was at a local pub in Ipswich, The Thomas Eldred, a very nice establishment in a very nice area. Even in those very early days I would try and localise the material and use gags that they could connect with.

There were condom machines in the pub toilets which were relatively new at the time and smartarses would write clever, witty graffiti on them:

My dad says they don't work!

Buy two, be one jump ahead!

Buy me and stop one!

Someone, somewhere wants a letter from you!

It's the worse chewing gum I have ever tasted!

Written on the skirting board below the machine.

Sex can stunt your growth!

Taking the mickey, excuse the pun, was nearly always a great way of making contact, however, there could sometimes be exceptions. There is a very thin line between friendly banter and insults. I would avoid certain words and getting too personal which could make the audience feel uncomfortable as well.

It was mainly stand-up to start with, no props or backing music, but this was about to change. Moving forward, I knew I wanted to use visual and vocal comedy to handle the more difficult challenges that lay ahead. I needed to get musical parts written and backing tapes produced to achieve this change. In those days we had cassette tapes. CD's, mini-discs and computers were not around then!

Anyway, that first show went really well, a local gig in a nice pub and everybody was willing me on to do well, being the boy next door so to speak.

Ad-libbing and dealing with hecklers would also play a part in making contact. Let's all hold hands and contact the living!

I said to the Barman, "A pint, a pie and a few kind words please." He replied, "Don't eat the pie!"

A bloke in the toilets stood beside me and said, "I'm proud of this." I said, "You should be, you're holding mine!"

A fella in the audience was wearing checked trousers. I said, "Does Rupert know you've got his trousers on?"

Is that your tie Sir or have you been sick?

And to anyone who looked scruffy:

How did you get past Bonfire Night?

Keep walking about, you'll sell that shirt!

Did you get dressed in the dark?

We are now talking over thirty-six years ago remember, and the down to earth humour seems so basic compared to the more edgier and punchier observational material that is performed today. Obviously, so much has changed in many facets because of the more modern and technological age we now live in. I had to start somewhere, it's not that I had served a full apprenticeship in Comedy. I went straight in at the deep end, sink or swim; I'm still not a very good swimmer today so I had to work hard and learn fast.

I was to learn very quickly what a tough game Comedy is. It can be a very jealous business full of criticism whether you are good or bad and I did learn one important thing though - if you cannot handle rejection, do not be a Comic.

Although content was important and you have a natural ability to make people laugh, I had to ask myself if I would be able to handle the pressure when the going got tough with tougher audiences and even tougher venues.

I look back and wonder how and where I found the drive and determination to get through some hard experiences in this highly competitive industry. Future work would come along sometimes through word of mouth and return bookings. However, too many bad days at the office and your career could be well and truly over before it really got going. As I said, you had to learn fast and I did.

John became a typical Agent in the sense that no matter how bad or tough the gig might be or how far I had to travel, he would make it sound like it would be so well worth going and a major plus for me. He was a smooth operator, I think that's the word, but persuasive may be better!

He said, "I've got a gig for you." I said, "Don't you threaten me John!"

Agents hate Acts because we take 85% of their money!

A female starlet, wanting to better herself in show business, saunters up to a reputable Agent at a showbiz function and asks, "Why don't I take you back to my room and we can spend the night together?" He replies, "What's in it for me?!"

After my debut as a paid solo performer John had secured a second gig at the very well to do Savoy Restaurant in Norwich City Centre through Norwich Artists, a reputable agency in the region. Coincidentally, Brian Russell, who ran the agency, was on the panel of judges at the Maltings New Faces talent final in Stowmarket. It was because of this that he was willing to give me a chance and help get me a foothold in the business at this very upmarket venue.

I am now on £50, only my second gig and I have got a 150% pay rise – not bad and that was the good news! It was a difficult night to say the least. The Savoy was a Greek Restaurant and it was small and held about fifty guests. It was straight after the meal with the atmosphere very laid back and there was me still trying to cut my teeth and get my act together. Although a bit raw in my approach, visual content was to be the flavour of the day! I found out hard and fast that visual and vocal comedy, impressions and impersonations would be a better ingredient at certain venues.

In today's world it has turned around somewhat and stand up is at the forefront of the act. The two can come together now and again, especially when you are performing on ships for example. The restaurant atmosphere was very low key as you can imagine, straight after a meal. There were only a few tables and it would have been very difficult at the best of times, let alone at the start of my new part-time career. Most of the material I had done to date, and that wasn't very much, was down to earth but now squeaky clean was needed.

I asked for Mussels, and the Doorman came over!

I said to the Waiter, "The steaks are much better and cheaper back in the USA." He replied, "Yes, but think of the airfares!"

I thought one of the prawns disagreed with me. I said they were expensive, he said they weren't!

I asked the Waitress, "Can I have a quickie?" She slapped me in the face! The man beside me said, "The word is Quiche!"

The Waitress said, "Excuse me, your husband is sliding down the chair." The lady replied, "No, my husband is now walking into the Restaurant!"

I didn't do these lines at the gig but I wish I had because I died on my proverbial arse!

I can remember that The Savoy was not the best of venues for me at that very early stage but as time went by I improved and returned to perform there again. Yes, they had me back and it was much better using more appropriate material.

Experience is everything!

Today I do enjoy the challenge of the more up market gigs, SAGA cruising, Cunard and the more refined corporate events.

I still had no idea that this comedy lark would actually become a career move even though the performing was starting to feel so natural to me. Finding the right material for each particular venue was essential.

Chapter Ten

Highs and Lows

For the next eighteen months or so the newly named Micky Zany would be treading the boards as a semi-professional, working five days a week in the proper job and then being Mr Funny Guy in his spare time. Many different challenges lay ahead and because of the day-time work, weekends were usually the only time to get away other than to local events. There was one such weekend in Nottingham, which included the Musters Nightclub and a similar weekend in the Midlands at the well renowned Barn Social Club in Aston, Birmingham.

I now experienced my first Hen Night. When it comes to letting off steam I think women are much worse than men. Male Strippers, a Drag Queen and yours truly compering. It was loud, bawdy but fun and the material for the girls had to be obvious, near the knuckle, saucy and spicy, well that's what they came for surely? No, not really, 'King Dick' was the star attraction for them!

A girl sat on Pinocchio's nose and said, "Tell me a lie!"

A girl said, "Mum, were you a flirt when you were younger?" She replied, "Yes, course I was." The girl asked, "Did you get punished?" She said, "Yes, I ended up with your father!"

At the Zoo, looking at the Elephants, the son said to the father, "What's that big thing hanging down there Dad?" The father replied, "That's the trunk son." He said, "No, not that, the other big thing?" "That's his tail son." "No, that big thing. I asked mother and she said it was nothing?" The father replied, "That's the trouble with your mother, she's been bloody spoilt!"

There was much work back then and most pubs and clubs had entertainment and variety shows as well. With only the two TV channels people would go out more and pay a small amount to see live entertainment. I worked many of the local establishments in my surrounding area, the bread and butter gigs that all became good ground work for me. I did my first radio interview with the lovely

Anthea Clarke, from Radio Suffolk, who had also been a panelist on that first solo talent show. Me on the radio. Mum was chuffed! Most of the venues in Ipswich are still around today and it is such a shame that they don't book many cabaret acts anymore, and they include:

Clapgate Lane Conservative Club
Gainsborough Labour Club
The Duke of Gloucester Pub
Bridgeward Social Club
Westgate Ward Social Club
Kesgrave Social Club
California Social Club
Kirby Street Conservative Club
Marlborough Bowls Club
Rosary Club......and many more.

Having a pop at the local Constabulary is always very well received even when working at their social club on their own patch.

A Policeman found a dead horse in 'The Buttermarket'. He couldn't spell Buttermarket so he dragged it into Queen Street!

I could see the Police car following me. One of nature's best laxatives is a blue light flashing!

He stopped and asked, "Where are we off to then?" I replied, "It will have to be your place, my wife's at home!"

He asked, "Why are you driving so fast?" I said, "I am going to a lecture." He said, "A lecture, at two in the morning?" I said, "You haven't met my wife have you!"

"Have you checked your tyres lately?" he asked. I got out and said, "One, two, three, four – yes, they're all there!"

He said, "Your brake light is not working." I got out and kicked the bumper and it came on. He said, "Now kick your windscreen, your Tax might come up as well!"

As the year came to a close I had a long week-end in Wales...Wales! It seemed a million miles away but I found the three venues there to be very friendly and successful. They were Sully Plastics on Barry Island, Rhydanna Sports Club and Trallwn Community Centre.

I went back to South Wales many times in those early days and the reaction was always positive, even at Swansea Dockers! I went there twice and Cumfellin Social Club on a Sunday evening which was known as the Comics Graveyard. I remember those days with great affection, I do love a good funeral!

My wife fell off the Welsh flag!

I love Wales. I saw Moby Dick three times!

They say, "Look youuu," and when you do there is nobody there!

There was a knock on the door in the village and the wife answered. A man said, "Some things have gone missing from the Pit and we believe Dai could be involved." The wife replied, "No, no, no, Dai wouldn't do that." The man said, "We would still like to speak to him." Then she said, "He's down the bottom of the garden, it's very muddy so you might want to take the conveyor belt!"

Localising gags is always important. I wanted to build routines about anything and everything that would involve the audience I was playing to at the time. I also liked making myself the butt of the gag using self-deprecating humour.

It was all a learning curve and it has taken many years for me to get to a place where I feel comfortable and confident with my material and content. I had to believe in that content, trying to be original was also important. As time has gone by I have found it easier, probably because of the experience I have gained, and the many real life observations have helped.

After Wales I had more confidence but I was about to be brought back down to earth again with a bump, a bloody big bump! If Wales was going to be well remembered with great affection then the North East was certainly not. Show business is a great leveller even then at my embryonic stage.

I left Pauline and Claire and the warmth and comfort of my village home near Ipswich, to drive up to the North East. I was booked for the Friday at South Shields Working Men's Club and I had to find digs which turned out to be a bed and breakfast sharing with two Irish navvies who were working on a building site nearby. What am I doing here I thought? I didn't need this. I remember sleeping, well trying to, with my money in my sock, hoping I wouldn't get mugged or worse! I was very green and very new to all this and I had nothing to compare it with. I hadn't travelled this far from home before either. Something told me that if I wanted to progress in the business then there would have to be times like this. I didn't know anything different and it was soul destroying at the time and I hadn't even got to the gig yet!

It sounds like a joke I know, a scene from a sitcom, sharing a room with two rough and ready geezers. It was no laughing matter and worse was to come. The Club was the gig from Hell. Nobody laughed! I can't remember what I did, and I don't want to. It wouldn't have mattered what I did, they still would not have laughed, maybe it was the language barrier! Southern bastard!

I didn't stay to do the Bishop Auckland or Sunderland gigs, I wanted to get back to planet earth! I seriously thought at the time about giving it up and do I need all this? To be honest, if I had gone back there ten years later with lots more experience and a better act it would still have been a bad experience as they will always be a tough audience to crack.

It mattered not; there they were reading their newspapers, playing dominoes, waiting for the Bingo. Nothing! I was so glad to get home, back to the land of the living where people gave you a chance.

Not much happened after the North East Welcome Club! I was still working locally in other clubs and there were plenty of them, all wanting a piece of the action! John was doing a fine job getting me lots of local work, he obviously felt that I had to get the North East nightmare out of my system as quickly as possible. We went to the Ipswich Rotary Club, The Aylesbourne Priory Caravan Park, Felixstowe Dock Club, The Golden Hind Pub and a couple of hotels thrown in as well which made it all seem worthwhile again, and not a Domino in sight!

Ad libs to the audience regarding their attire:

I see you have sacrificed fashion for comfort!

Nice suit Sir. When are you going for your second fitting?!

It looks like you have been to the Jumble Sale after everyone else has bought the good stuff.

He was wearing a black and white spotted shirt and I asked, "Do you keep Pigeons?"

Is it fancy dress – what have you come as?

I was in the loo, the man next to me said, "You're holding yours with all four fingers." I said, "Yes, three of them are getting wet!"

It was just a bit of sauce and spice, cheeky but nice, not pretentious. They were out for a good laugh and friendly banter was all part of it – both ways I hasten to add! I could take as good as I gave. I liked the audience having a go, as long as it was friendly, it was always extra laughs for the act! They were still working class venues but the people liked to laugh and were not afraid to enjoy themselves.

What was on the horizon was the holiday camp circuits, the likes of Butlins, Pontins, Warners and Haven. It was now Spring and I was off again on my travels. It had been nearly four months since that cold journey to the North East, and I was so glad to go to Puckpool and St. Clare on the Isle of White for Warner Holiday Centres. I was hoping this would be a lot warmer, especially the weather and the reception. It was quite a drive, then onto the ferry and back home after the Sunday night show for my day job on the Monday morning!

I suppose looking back, it was a kind of adventure, not only finding my way in the business but finding my way around the country, there were no Sat Navs or M25 then. A second trip to South Wales followed staying in pro digs in Cathedral Road, Cardiff, with the Welsh agent Don Tyrer. He was known as The Godfather, and his lovely wife Betty cooked for all and sundry. It was great there, lots of artists stayed and it was nice to bond and find a camaraderie amongst fellow travellers. Don was a hard man, I think he was an ex miner but he was loveable. Why he was called the Godfather I am not quite sure; maybe if you didn't do too well or died on your arse then when you woke up in the morning there would be a horse's head on the pillow! He once fell asleep beside the fire with his foot in it, what a muppet, we laughed, Don didn't though! He used to come to the gigs with me now and again and he was good company and he knew the business inside out. There was a little bit of extra pressure with him being there but he was always on hand to give me advice.

If I were you I'd take a few weeks off son, then quit for good!

My advice to him was to get a fireguard!

Then came Butlins at Barry Island, Swansea Dockers and Tenby, you couldn't get much further West than Tenby. I was beginning to think that John Clown was a frigging travel agent! Swansea Dockers is renowned as a tough gig but they not only let me live, they asked me back...they couldn't believe it the first time! I am not blowing my own trumpet because I can't play one but it was a really good feeling to go back to such a venue. I found it was a help to tell gags in their own Welsh accent, it seemed to work especially when the accent was not very good. I could pick up accents quickly and I gradually built up routines around various regions up and down the country.

They sing, 'We'll Keep a Welcome in the Hillside'. But they won't let you in their houses!

I said to this one fella, "There are two good things to come out of Wales, rugby players and loose women." This angry fella replied, "My wife is Welsh." I replied, "What team does she play for?!"

There were two Welsh lads in a pub, a blonde walks in and one of the lads said to her, "Tickle your arse with a feather?" She replied rather sternly, "I beg your pardon?" He said, "Particularly nice weather." The lad repeats this with another lady who walks in the pub. Then his mate, who is slightly drunk, asks him, "What was that all about?" The lad replies, "If the lady is not up for it you get round it by saying something else." A brunette now walks into the pub and the other lad drunkenly says to her, "Stick a feather up your arse!" She replies very sternly, "I beg your pardon?" and the drunk lad said, "It's pissing down outside!"

Another talent show was on offer next but this time it was a much more prestigious programme, BBC TV's Rising Stars. Unfortunately, I had no joy, I was nowhere near good enough yet. I was not ready and still had so much to learn. I was not even professional – but that was all about to change.

Chapter Eleven

Turning Pro

It was now early 1980 and I auditioned for a very well known Midland impresario, Billy 'Cocker' Forrest. He looked like Danny Devito, the penguin in one of the Batman films. What a character; he was a typical agent.

Are you Jewish......not necessarily!

The audition was at The Trocadero Club in Nuneaton early one morning. It was a very cold audition, not so much in weather terms but just a few acts hanging around with him and his staff judging. When it came to my turn I was three minutes into my set when the man himself stood up and halted the proceedings. I generally thought that I had blown it, failing miserably, but I was wrong. On the contrary, he said he liked me and wanted to offer me a Summer Season in Jersey! The contract would be six months long and Jersey was considered at that time to be the cream of places to work. There were ten static production shows and four travelling shows on the island as well as the in house entertainers.

Billy had two of the travelling shows and there was I passing a three minute audition to go to a place I knew nothing about, I probably didn't even know where it was at the time!

It was going to be a tough decision to make, six months away from home and the family, giving up a very good steady job and all the trimmings that went with it, to go into the fickle world of show business.

I must admit that when I got there I fell in love with the island and have since worked and travelled there many times.

That season in 1980 was to kick-start my professional career. It was a giant step to take and a really big decision to make. My wife Pauline played a big part and was very positive about me going and I think she could see that this was a really big break for me. She helped make the decision a lot easier to be fair and if she had been against it I would not have gone and I wonder how the last thirty or so years would have panned out.

I headlined this one travelling show and a Liverpool Comic, Joey Kaye, was to headline the sister show. I left my proper job at the end of April and the following night I did my first pro gig at the local Gainsborough Labour Club in Ipswich and three days later I was on the ferry to Jersey. I was excited of course and glad to be working with other acts in a show every night making it all the more appealing. The prospect of being a Comedian full-time was very satisfying and I wanted to get as much visual, vocal and stand-up material into the act to cope with the many different challenges that lay ahead.

As my stage name suggests the act needed to be full of off the wall interaction as well as stand up and gag telling. There were some really good venues but also a few tricky ones. The worst part was leaving home and not seeing my family for some time although they came over as much as possible, mainly in the school holidays. Their first trip to the island had almost devastating consequences though.

The drive to Southend Airport, where they were to fly from, was going fine until the driver in front decided to overtake without looking. Pauline's mum Jane was driving and could not avoid hitting the central reservation due to the driver in front of them overtaking without indicating. The car rolled over several times and there were no seat belt laws in those days and no belt in the back of the car. Claire was thrown out of the car on impact, however she was remarkably unscathed.

I knew nothing about the accident until they got to Jersey as they kept it from me and said their flight was delayed for some reason. The next day, when they came through the the arrival hall in Jersey, Pauline and Jane had minor injuries, cuts and bruises. Claire, who was three years old at the time, was absolutely fine and there was not a mark on her. It could have been so much worse but God was on our side that day and I dread to think of what might have happened.

The first gig at the five star De La Plage Hotel, just outside St. Helier, was probably the hardest gig of them all and to be honest it was a nightmare. We performed at two different venues each night, seven nights a week for the whole six month season. Billy said originally, "Don't worry, the hotels are next door to each other." They were, but unfortunately, we did not work them on the same night!

We would set the gear up for the first show, do the show, strip the gear down, pack up and travel to the next venue. This could be a fifteen to twenty minute drive and then set it all up again and do the second show, strip down and that was that. The first show would be around 9.00 pm and the second around 11.00 pm. I thought to myself, welcome to show business, we did more spots than a welder!

At that time I would open up wearing a leopard skin coat and a ginger wig and tail, a sort of Rod Stewart look alike. It's fair to say that it must have been a little bit over the top for the De La Plage, it was certainly not the place for my wacky, off the wall humour. More whiter than white sedate stand-up was what was needed. Some of the other places loved the visual content and it took a while to suss them all out and I learnt fast. I had to!

There were two holiday centres and many friendly hotels where the show would go really well: Pontins at Plemont Bay, The Jersey Holiday Village, The Modern Hotels, The Merton, Le Coie, Silver Springs, Norfolk Lodge, Chelsea, Angleterre, Westhill, Golden Sands, Normandy, Bayview, Hermitage, to name but a few. There would also be a sprinkling of French people in the audience at one or two places which was not good for a stand-up Comedian, so some visual was needed here I thought!

I went out with a French girl once, what do you call those French girls? ....
Baguettes!

McDonalds in America; Big Mac, large fries and a coke. McDonalds in France; Frogs legs, French fries and a Perrier!

I enjoyed the shows from start to finish and learnt so much, I never tired of my first professional contract despite the number of shows and no nights off. It was my first full season and I grabbed it with both hands and I have worked there in many summer seasons since. It has become almost a second home to me.

We did fourteen shows a week for twenty-six weeks and it took a lot of hard work and resilience but most of all the Company were great and we all got on extremely well. We had a great male singer called Titch Cooper, and four girl singers; not all in one go I hasten to add. It was a tough season with fourteen shows a week and not all of them could handle the pace! We were well supported by a very talented backing duo, Alex and Graham. Jersey was a great place to be at that particular time and I made many friends and I felt very lucky that I had such a wonderful place to kick start my professional career. It was almost six years before I went back to work in Jersey but I visited every year to see friends who lived and worked on the island.

Some of the artists that performed there in 1980 were: Joe Longthorne, Colin Crompton, Bryn Philips and Lee Clark at the Hotel De France in St. Helier. David Copperfield, Leah Bell and Tony Maiden at the New Mediterranean Hotel in St. Ouen. Micky Gunn and Renato (before Renee) were at the Sunshine Hotel in St. Helier. Kenny Smiles and The Rocking Berries appeared at Behan's in West Park and Stuart Gillies and Pat Mooney were at Ceasars Palace at Greve De Lecq. Pat Mooney started the Monday Club that year, raising funds for the Variety Club of Jersey.

All these years on and how times have changed. There are no production or travelling shows now, just a few in house hotel performers and The Jersey Opera House. Later, impresario Dick Ray was to become instrumental in my career by producing five fantastic seasons that I appeared in at the famous Caesars Palace.....in Jersey!

After turning professional in 1980 there was considerable work in all sorts of places. In those early days a lot of the material was second hand but gradually I would be putting together my own bits and pieces. The act was down to earth but so were most of the venues and everybody has to start somewhere. I was a quick learner and I did not want to do what the other comics were doing. As with all the top quality acts, I needed my own identity and style to be seen to have the originality that would make me stand out.

As time went by I was starting to do this and get my own act together so to speak. Thinking of lines, being inventive and creating off-the-wall impressions and situations was starting to take shape but there was still a long way to go.

After the summer season working in Jersey every night, I decided that I would never do that heavy workload again but at the time of going professional it was the start of a journey. It was because of that length of contract that I obtained my Equity card and I am still a member today. I wasn't quite sure why, but later on when television work beckoned, membership of Equity was essential.

Anglia TV came calling on several occasions. I don't mean on my front door, I was asked to do some TV and film work. There were no leading parts, not even a speaking role, just extra work and walk-ons. I did have a speaking part once when I was asked a question on set, but instead of saying 'yes' they told me to just nod. The bastards! It could have been the start of a flourishing film career!

Sylvester Stallone as Humpty Dumpty, "Hey, don't push me!"

Sean Connery's agent said, "I have an audition tomorrow morning for you Sean, be there for tennish." Sean replied, "Tennish, I haven't even got a racket?"

Whatever happened to the Elephant Man. One good film, haven't seen him since?

Forrest Gump is doing an advert for condoms. "Mama said, if you don't use one, you never know what you're gonna get!"

Hannibal Lectar went on a cruise and was asked at the dinner table, "Would you like to see the menu Sir?" He replied, "No, just give me the passenger list!"

I have seen all of Bruce Willis's films except the one, and that was the hit blockbuster Armageddon. Still, it's not the end of the world is it?!

In those heady days of the early eighties, work was constant and I was starting to build a reputation for myself. I am and always have been my own biggest critic and I set my standards very high, too high sometimes. I always wanted to be as good as the best, nothing wrong with that. As a famous film actor once said, I think on Wogan many years ago, and I believe it was Kirk Douglas, "You must always strive for perfection even though you never get there."

Sometimes, I might go really well on stage but still not be happy for one reason or another! I am thinking of new ideas constantly. It was important for me on many occasions to make an impact right from the start and grab the audience's attention early on and keep it. Some people have very short attention spans!

As I was headlining on many occasions this meant that I had to be good enough to follow quality acts, sometimes very funny ones, and audiences would occasionally be very noisy and volatile.......I blame the drink!

My act took me all over the UK as far afield as Scotland, Wales and Cumbria; The North East to The Midlands, Manchester to Mablethorpe, Kettering to Kent, Harefield to Herne Bay, Leicester to Lowestoft, Nottingham to Newquay, Bristol to Bournemouth and of course, a multitude of gigs in East Anglia.

The climate of today's entertainment industry is far removed from back in the eighties. Nowadays a more laid back approach is needed in some venues and on cruise ships, but when I was working those late night circuits, particularly Pontins and Butlins, where the punters were really up for it and a little the worse for drink, I had to be strong enough to cope. The clever patter would not be enough sometimes; however, what came next really helped me grab them from the off. It was something to shut them up, something loud. I know......an exploding guitar!

Chapter Twelve

The Big Bang Theory!

I was eager to find that elusive opening, not just a song but something that would blow the roof off, not literally obviously. I wanted to grab their attention from the start. As the stage name suggests I wanted to be as Zany as I could, so with the help and expertise of my then brother-in-law Dave, who was by trade an Electrician, we thought of producing this grand opening. As it turned out it was a marvellous idea but not without its early setbacks.

I had to get a guitar and take the front off very carefully with a Stanley knife, then replace it with a replica front made out of fibreglass and line the inside of the shell of the guitar with fibreglass as well. We installed a switch attached to a battery connected to an exploding Maroon inside the guitar and with the use of small magnets on the inside of the front and the base of the guitar we put the front back on which was held together by these magnets.

The trial explosion did not go exactly to plan as the connections on the battery were on the wrong way round. Therefore, before we could even put the front back on the guitar and press the switch, the Maroon went off! We were inside Dave's garden shed which nearly collapsed with the deafening noise and it was a few days before our hearing came back!

For ten years this prop became the opening of my act, not for every gig though for obvious reasons, but it set the tone and made sense of the billing...Micky Zany! Adding funny props and visual comedy gave me that extra buzz I wanted. I had to be careful when choosing the venues where I could use it and setting it up before going on stage. It was always one of those close your eyes moments!

Two long weekends in the Midlands for the Bernard Parr Agency and I was now on a whopping £100 a gig. It was the same year that Trevor Francis became the first million pound footballer. Not quite in the same league but it felt like it!

Local gigs were plentiful; social and sports clubs, village halls, even schools were popping up and of course hotel functions.

One such hotel was the Grand Hotel at Felixstowe, not far from me. It sounded grand but it was more of a guest house! I'd spent my youth at the seaside in Felixstowe, on the pier and in the amusements arcades. I could relate to the area and had amassed a number of amusing stories.

I had my first sexual experience on the roller-coaster in Felixstowe....I was on my own!

It was considered to be a more reserved seaside town and is still a place where you might go to live when you retire.

When you get to sixty-five in Ipswich, they put you on a coach and they move you to Felixstowe – it's the law!

It's a year on and I'm back at the Savoy Restaurant in Norwich. This time with more experience and hopefully better material, or rather material more suited to the venue. I started to work on routines that would suit Norfolk especially as I was working in that area more and more.

Doing a survey in a village in Norfolk, a Researcher knocked on one door and asked the man, "Where does the oldest inhabitant live in the village?" The man replied, "We don't have one, he died last week!"

"What is the death rate in the village?" "One per person!"

Signs on the roadside: 'End of roundabout' and 'Wasn't that a bad bend back there!'

"What's the quickest way to the Village Hall?" "Are you driving or on foot?" "Driving." "That's the quickest way!"

"Are you local?" "Yes, I'm standing right here!"

"How do you get to the Village Hall?" "I go with my brother."

"You're not much help!" "Well at least I ain't lost!"

Believe it or not I found myself back in the North East. I must have taken a wrong turning!

John, my Agent, did a fair bit of work up there with the band so obviously thought, because of the contacts he had made, it would be a great idea to give me a second go at it. What a plonker!

On paper, good. In practice, shit!

Walker Social Club in Newcastle on a Sunday lunchtime and then Hartlepool Boilermakers on a Monday night in November. The audience were colder than the weather and it was frigging freezing up there! I was watching dead people sit up!

I even tried to pull myself off, (no, not in that sense) after the first of two spots, but the concert Secretary said; "Nah way bonnie lad, nobody talked, you kept their attention, they loved ya!" I did the two nights then came home. I decided that me and the North East were just not compatible. The relationship was over. It was back to show business. Still, it stopped me getting bigheaded – it was like working on radio!

Where would you be without a laugh? The North East!

I had an unbelievable first year as a professional. A Summer Season on the beautiful Island of Jersey, and many varied gigs. I made a welcome return to my first pro venue, The Thomas Eldred Pub, also Sizewell Nuclear Power Station, RAF Wattisham, Harlow Police, John Players and Fisons at Ipswich and another great weekend back in Wales.

Variety is the spice of life they say and it was certainly turning out to be. Whereas the North East was not too fruitful for me (that's one way of putting it) – Scotland was the opposite!

After a weekend in Cumbria, Workington and Whitehaven, I travelled north of the border to do a week in bonnie Scotland for a loveable Agent, Andy 'Times are Hard' Green.

Andy had seen me in the travelling show in Jersey when he was staying at the Monterrey Hotel.

I did eight shows in seven days including venues such as Hearts and Hibernian Football Clubs, St. Mirren, Rosyth Naval Base in Fife, (where the bananas come from!) and many other friendly fire clubs.

I stayed in digs with Andy's daughter and her husband and they made me very comfortable. When I look back to the days of pro digs I wonder how I did it! In today's world I would never do that. I'm too much of a home boy and don't travel very far at all, unless it's on a cruise ship!

Cruising takes me away nowadays, sometimes up to twenty weeks a year, but it is a very different environment to those clubby days back then.

January in Scotland doesn't feel very appealing now. Back then I was starting off and had nothing to fear or so I thought!

I went to Glasgow for a laugh and came back in stitches!

Why do they keep their money in their Sporrans? If they get mugged they enjoy it!

Do Scottish people come from a Scotch egg?!

To know what Clan they're from? Put your hand up his kilt and if he's got a quarter pounder, he's a McDonald!

Two Scots walk into a pub and start eating their sandwiches. The Landlord says, "You can't eat your own food in here." So they swopped!

They found a wage packet and one said: "Look at the Tax he's paid?!"

Some comedians in those days would take, borrow or nick material but as time went by I found it so important to put my own stamp and interpretation on things. I was trying to think of new fresh lines and ideas constantly and eventually have an act with as much originality in it as possible.

Sometimes, others might watch you and take some of the material. I never worried about that and it made me want to write more gags and routines. You've got to keep moving with the times.

You sometimes hear the expression, if it's not broken, don't fix it. Personally, I am constantly updating and improving my act to keep me on my toes. I have never wanted to work to a set script day in day out – or is it night in night out?

March saw me working with the very funny Jimmy 'Kinnel' Jones, a lovely comic, kind and generous. He would tell you a joke and then how to turn it around to suit your act. Jimmy was a real gag man and great at it but we differed in that I wanted to veer more toward the observational side of comedy. I was to work with him many times and I supported him on his first theatre tour, which wasn't too far away.

A three foot man went out with a seven foot women, but he had to jack it in!

A seven foot man went out with a three foot woman. He was nuts over her!

A Butcher said to a lady customer, "Pound of fillet?" She replied, "Pound you don't!"

"Can I have a torch dad?" "Why?" "I wanna go courting." "I never had a torch when I went courting." "Look what you ended up with!"

"Give me fifty pence dad and I'll tell you who mummy slept with when you were away last night." "Tell me that son and I will give you a pound." "It was me!"

"What's love juice dad?" "It's when mummy and daddy get close in bed and that's what we produce." "What's that got to do with Tennis?"

"If you do that son you'll go blind." "I'm over here dad!"

My contract with Johnny Walker (Aka Clown) came to an end, inevitable but mutual. I think we both saw it coming.

He made me feel special and was very inspiring. I suppose he didn't really know the right people to take me further maybe?

John had got me started three years earlier and I will always appreciate what he did for me, apart from sending me off to the North East, ha ha!

I hope one day we can meet and catch up.

Chapter Thirteen

Here, There and Everywhere!

I had an altercation with a toilet once!

I was gigging at King Richard Road Working Men's Club in Leicester and just before I went on stage I had to use the loo, pre-show nerves being how they are! I always get them, I now realise adrenalin is brown! As I rose from the loo the whole plumbing system came away from the wall, there was water everywhere! I was wearing my stage suit, a pink ultra-violet silky number and the water started soaking up my trousers, making its way up the legs like a thermometer! I heard the compere call out my name and I rushed on to the stage, drainpipe trousers and all!

The sight of this broke the ice straight away, excuse the pun, but I then had to announce over the PA system that someone needed to tend to the broken loo! They all thought I was joking and had just peed myself because I was so nervous! You had to be there!

I have to sit down every time I go to the loo – I mustn't lift anything heavy!

Scotland must have been a success as I was asked to return a month later. I didn't relish going away one little bit but I had this gut feeling inside telling me I had to do these places and travel somewhat in order to further my career and try to compete with the very best. I'm sure no entertainer or sportsman has ever made good by just working on their doorstep all their life. Besides, I had bills to pay and a family to support!

Bramford Football Club, near Ipswich, was my local village team and they asked me to perform at their local end of season dance. Local boy makes good…. luvley!

Shortly afterwards I was booked for a private function at the Rosetta Bar in Belfast. Yes, Belfast, Northern Ireland! This was probably my first corporate function, I cannot remember too much about the content, did I touch on Irish humour or not?

As it turned out they loved it. I did ask them first, about the material, I'm not stupid! I wouldn't choose to do the same lines today, nothing to do with PC. There comes a time when you move on and leave them well behind, or sometimes turn lines around so I would become the butt of the gag.

To fly to Belfast for a one nighter and come back intact made me feel extra special. It gave me an extra lift and I realised even more so that I had to keep expanding the material to cope with all these diverse bookings.

If you play golf in Northern Ireland, do not mention you are gonna hit a provisional!

A man walks into a Pub on his own and asks the Barman, "Can I have three pints of lager please?" The Barman said, "Three pints, you're thirsty?" The man replied, "No, one is for me and the other two are for my two mates." This goes on for a week. The week after the man asks for only two pints. "Oh dear," said the Barman, "Has one of your mates passed away?" He said, "No, I'm on antibiotics, so I'm off the beer!"

"Is that the Sun up there?" "I don't know, I don't live around here!"

"Did you see the eclipse?" "No, the moon got in the way!"

He saw a sign saying:-Boxer dogs for sale. He asked the owner, "How many dogs in the box?"

Around this busy time there were many venues that were springing up here, there and everywhere. Knights at the Barking Fox was a nightclub restaurant not too far from Ipswich and certain named acts would top the bill. I supported some of them on several occasions including; Lennie Henry, Mike Reid and Lennie Bennett. Another regular was the Old Orchard Restaurant at Harefield in Hertfordshire. It was a wonderful cabaret restaurant, very intimate and it would be a venue where many of the comics would double up after a booking earlier in the evening.

Harefield Hospital is remembered for the pioneering heart transplants at the time.

I had so many diverse gigs in so many diverse places and the miles I travelled!

I felt at times that comics were long distance drivers who told jokes at the end of each drive! There were so many funny things that would happen along the way and they would become installed in the act and stay there, even today.

At Loudwater British Legion, west of London, I was well into the act and about to do an Indian routine, feathered Indian, I hasten to add. To start the routine I asked the ageing drummer for Indian drum beats. He wasn't the sharpest tool in the box bless him, he missed my cue and I went with my mouth: Boom, boom boom boom; Boom, boom boom boom. To which he responded with his mouth: Boom, boom boom boom; Boom, boom boom boom.

I shouted out, "Use your sticks you daft bugger!" It got a massive laugh from the audience so I kept it in the act and still do it today albeit in a different way. The Red Indian routine is well gone, although it was very funny in its time.

What do you call a bloke who hangs around with musicians? A Drummer!

I would like to thank some great musicians but they haven't turned up!

Without these guys – I'd have been brilliant!

They have played under a great handicap, they're sober!

Meet the Symbolics: there's Sym on the drums and……..!

Here's the backing trio; Mr. Still, Mr. Novak and Mr. Good….. they are Still, Novak and Good!

Wales and the South West became familiar territory for me. It was good work down there in the clubs, hotels and holiday centres. One such notable gig was the Gold Diggers Club in Chippenham, Wiltshire. I can recall with great fondness supporting the fabulous Sounds of the Platters.

My early memories of my dad playing their LP on our Dansette record player came flooding back. I knew all the words to all the songs. Herb Reid was the only remaining survivor but it was such a great thrill to be working with them.

It was at this time that showcases would be the place for you to cameo your repertoire so that agents and bookers could come and see you and hopefully book you for their venues.

More often than not, members of the public would be there as well, this was obviously a big plus and that would be where the bulk of the laughter would come from....hopefully! Also Watneys would sponsor variety shows in the pubs and clubs in the South, these were a joy to do, with other acts on the bill and a backing band thrown in as well. As time went by and the act was getting stronger, I found myself topping the bill.

My act was developing with visual and vocal comedy high on the list which was especially needed in some of the venues. I used lots of props in those days and with the advantage of the exploding guitar the impact was there. I would use either the opening line from John Miles 'Music' or 'My Way' by Frank Sinatra… and now the end is near…bang!

Closing the show would generally be the hardest spot, by this time a lot of the audience would be well juiced up. Watneys drinks would be greatly reduced in price so as to promote their beers. All in all you had to get their attention quickly and keep the pace going. I found that dying on my arse was not an option, I would get out there and give 'em what for!

Obviously, on less exuberant nights with a more sedate audience I could tone it down. The exploding guitar would not be on the menu unless they were asleep of course!

In today's world nearly all of those props have gone, along with most of the venues unfortunately! Now stand-up takes the lead but I still use the band with off the wall humour and throw away vocal comedy and parodies, originality being the key.

Local shows were in great abundance. It seemed that most of the Social Clubs had cabarets then, but very rarely nowadays which is a great shame. There would be the Braintree Barn, the Copford Windmill, where I had watched other comics over ten years earlier, and holiday centres along the Essex coast, the likes of St Osyth, Point Clear and Seawick.

It was around now that Stag and Hen nights became a regular feature on the circuit. This meant that my material had to be, shall we say, more edgy, risqué, spicier or is bluer the word I am looking for?

Being the compere to an all-male audience, some very inebriated, called for much stronger material and the ability to have endless ad libs to deal with the hecklers! I didn't want to be too aggressive.....I liked my face the way it was!

As she lay down on the couch the Doctor immediately had sex with her and said

63

afterwards, "That's my problem solved, what's yours?" She replied, "VD!"

A Swedish girl was going to marry an English boy and she was not very good at English speaking. She asks the Doctor, "What is the long thing called between his legs?" The Doctor said, "That is the Penis." She repeats, "The Penis. What is the round piece at the end of the Penis called?" "That is the bell end." replied the Doctor. She repeats, "The bell end. What are those two round things eighteen inches back from the bell end called?" The Doctor said, "For your sake, I hope they are the cheeks of his arse!"

Heckles:

I won't take the mickey, natures done it for me!

I'd shake your hand but you're using it!

I bet you don't say a lot at home!

Ignorance is bliss. He must be ecstatic!

He's trying to produce a joke like his mum and dad did!

A night out for him. A night off for his family!

Hen nights could be much worse, a bunch of drunken women waiting to see the obvious, and it wasn't the comic! It was mind blowing at times!

Chapter Fourteen

The Second Coming........It's a Boy!

In May of 1982 I joined Barry Dye Management, a well-respected local Agent in Ipswich. He had worked the circuits with his band and had many contacts and looked after several acts and artists.

It proved to be a fruitful relationship, and the next few years saw me move from the rank and file to the bigger and better venues including TV, theatre and cruising. It was at this time, that Barry first spotted the raw talent of a young Shane Richie whilst holidaying at the Pontins Centre in Torremolinos. Shane was a Bluecoat back then and when he came home to the UK, Barry took him under his wing. So with myself and Shane, Maxwell Plumb, Chris North, Paul Zenon, and Simon Lovell, Barry had accumulated a stable of talented performers, and the eighties was a very busy time for us all.

I was working every Sunday at the Butlins Holiday Centre at the Crazy Horse Saloon in Clacton-on-Sea in Essex. My great friend John Booth was with me, he came to the odd gig with me now and again and he still does today. It's nice to have a bit of company now and then and it makes the journey go quicker.

On Sunday the thirteenth of June 1982 I got home from the gig and Pauline was waiting, bag in hand, to go to the hospital. The next day our son James was born, it was another fantastic moment, being there to see the birth of our second child, as with Claire! When I see that 'Only Fools and Horses' episode with Del Boy holding Damien saying, "It's a....it's a...it's a ....baby!" I always think of that day. Soppy old sod!

That night, mother and baby were doing fine in hospital and dad went off to work at a Watney's Roadshow in South Oxney, near Watford.

I was so elated, a girl and now a boy, wow! The show that night was a bit special to say the least, I had the whole audience wet the baby's head, fantastic!

I was so happy having a boy and a girl, how lucky I was and to this day they have done me proud. I love them unconditionally.

On a special note, on the day James was born the Argie's surrendered over the Falklands war. I don't think his coming had anything to do with it though!

I was now starting to work at the major nightclubs around the country, including the likes of Newmarket Cabaret Club, Baileys at Watford and the Golden Garter at Wythenshawe, Manchester. These were great venues for me where the stars used to top the bill.

Newmarket Cabaret Club in Suffolk, was to become a regular haunt and just before it was refurbished that year I performed there with Bernard Manning. I remember this gig mainly for the fact that it was the terrible day when HMS Sheffield went down in the South Atlantic.

Baileys at Watford was a great venue, very vibrant and I loved working there, supporting many top acts. The first weeks included, Jimmy Jones, Mike Reid and once again the outrageous Bernard Manning.

At the Golden Garter in Wythenshawe, Manchester, I worked with a band called Toto Coelo, they had a one hit wonder with 'I Eat Cannibals!' Anyone remember? No, you're not the only ones! It was like a furniture exhibition, a neighbourhood watch! We all had to join hands to contact the living! There is an art in dying with grace......I called it rehearsing!

More prestigious gigs were starting to come my way. Another special was at Lakeside Country Club and a benefit night for Lennie Peters of Peters and Lee fame and the song 'Welcome Home'. Jim Davidson was the host and very funny he was may I say, Chas and Dave, Lyn Paul, ex New Seeker, a fine original and very funny comedy act called Ben Murphy, and myself.

I opened the second half after Jim had warmed them up for me (ha ha!). He was always full of energy and near the knuckle and everybody loved it in those days. I went the other way and kept it clean, I was more than pleased with my performance and so were the audience.

There have been many special nights when it has been different from the norm and when they come along you want to grab the moment and hope the publicity will get you bigger and better things in the future.

Hen nights were becoming much more popular, and I was being booked a lot probably because the act was very visual and musical with lots of impressions, impersonations and send ups. Such a format included the likes of Mick Jagger, Tom Jones, Worzel Gummidge, Elvis and others and would always win the girls over, those that weren't too out of it on drink that is! Clever stand-up was a waste of time at these events.

Some ladies would be more open-minded than others. There would usually be an element that would drink too much and often spoil it for the others. I did a hen party once at the Hammersmith Palais.

I thumped my neighbour for peeing his name in the snow in my garden – it was in my wife's handwriting!

When Fanny Craddock's cooking programme was on the telly she would show the viewers how to make the perfect Yorkshire puddings. Afterwards, husband Johnny once said on air, "Well ladies, I hope your puddings come out like Fanny's!"

My wife gave me oral sex last night – she sat on the bed and talked me out of it!

She stood there naked. I said, "You're going grey down there." She replied, "Grey! They're frigging cobwebs!"

I came home and caught the wife in bed with the Milkman. She said, "This was your idea. I asked you, shall I give the Milkman a £1 tip for Christmas? You said, "F**k the Milkman, give him fifty pence!"

The wife said to the husband, "I've had a shave down there and I've got a Brazilian, you know what that means?" He replied, "Yeh, the sink's blocked!"

The wife said, "I've got you a penis enlarger for your birthday." He opened the present and it was a magnifying glass!

He said, "Let's try a different position tonight my dear." She said, "OK, you do the ironing and I'll lay on the sofa farting all night!"

Mind you, the ladies nights could vary from the loud and boisterous at the Hammersmith Palais with lots of screaming women, to a more sedate atmosphere such as the White Lion pub in Aldeburgh, a very refined part of the country on the Suffolk coast. Sometimes a more laid back approach was needed, whereas at other times I had to go for it.

"Dad, mum says I come from a sugar bowl." "Yes, that's about the size of it!"

"Mummy, why can't I have one of those things that my little brother has got?" Mummy replied, "Don't worry, as long as you've got one of these you'll always

get one of those!"
"Our son's got whips and chains under his bed and he's reading about fetish and stuff." "Well, I can hardly give him a good hiding can I?"

A woman was in a shop doorway with her knickers round her ankles. When someone pointed this out she said, "Has he gone?"

A lady in the street had one boob hanging out and when someone told her she said, "Oh my God, I've left the baby on the bus!"

A fella knocks on the door and a lady answers. He said, "Hello love, I fancy you." "I beg your pardon," she replied. He said, "I'd like to take you to bed." Once again she said even more sternly, "I beg your pardon?" "I'll give you £200" he said. "Ok, come in," she happily replied. Later on her husband came home and asked, "Did George call round and leave my wages?"

To a big busted lady:

'If you fell over, you wouldn't break your nose!'

I won't come too close – I might fall in!

Are you two sisters? – Where's Cinderella!

It was very saucy and risque at times, it was horses for courses and nobody complained. The atmosphere would dictate the choice of material most of the time.

The different genres, from the social clubs to the nightclubs, the hens to the stags, the holiday centres to the corporates kept me on my toes, but then came the moment that would hopefully reward me for all the hard work I had put in to date.....or so I thought.

Chapter Fifteen

I'm on the Telly – Don't Fall Off!

Army bases were now having shows and these could be tough especially corporal or junior ranks. They weren't always the greatest of venues, or the most receptive of mobs, sorry - audiences. The more younger soldiers might be well bevvied, but lucky for me I had the experience of doing the stag and hen nights, but generally army bases weren't very enjoyable evenings. I had to take the friendly abuse sometimes, it was hard to keep a group of boisterous young lads quiet. I think they thought it was their perogative to heckle and join in. Barracks to them!

You can often learn from these experiences, I know it would be easier not to go back there, but it was often a challenge sometimes trying to find out the right format for all these difficult situations.

There were some really nice venues around but also some right sh….sh….. shabby ones as well! From Dagenham Working Mens Club to Baileys at Watford, from the Corporal's Mess at Colchester Garrison to the Old Orchard Restaurant at Harefield and from the Hammersmith Palais to the Aldeburgh White Lion. Variety is definitely the spice of life!

From time to time I would go back to the Maltings at Stowmarket in Suffolk where it all began. I felt confident now that I had some sort of act! It was good to go back and show my home crowd that it was well worth taking the risk in going professional.

Another fabulous venue was Victorias nightclub on the A20 at Harrietsham, near Maidstone in Kent. I performed there many, many times for over ten years and it was such a delight to work at that cabaret nightspot. Like many clubs and cabaret pubs of yesteryear, most have either become disco's or Tesco's now!

The Pontins circuit was next. Hemsby, the first centre I went to, was just up from Great Yarmouth. The one thousand seater night club called The Norfolk Bar hosted a darts weekend. It was electric, I loved it and received a standing ovation. There were no chairs in the room! Ha ha!

Dave Bond, aka Bondi, the Entertainments Manager, became a really good friend. I loved working the Norfolk Bar, it wasn't easy, you had to attack the audience rather than defend and not be laid back. When I came off that night Bondi was almost in tears. He was so proud, just like me. There are times when you feel you have come of age and that was one of those nights. I miss you Bondi.

I had lots of visual stuff and off the wall impressions in my act. It was fast, furious and manic. I had to go in strong, but I never swore and was never too blue. I went to the line but never crossed it.

Irish boxer in the ring, gets knocked down. His corner shouts out, "Stay down till nine. He shouts back, "What time is it now?"

My impression of a man with a plastic hip standing beside the fire......I FALL OVER !! (Visual gag)

I was gonna do an impression of a Jewish streaker....but there's no point!

Custer's Last Stand.
Custer was all on his own surrounded by 10,000 Indians. He suddenly sees a bottle and smashes it and out comes a Genie. The Genie said, "You can have three wishes but whatever you have the Indian's get two. If you want a gun, they have two guns; a cannon, they have two cannons." Custer says, "I'll have a glass eye!"

A young labourer was wearing Indian feathers on the building site. The Foreman had said he's getting rid of all the cowboys in the morning!

Another special was in the mix, and this one was extra special, my first TV appearance! Barry had arranged an audition for a Tyne Tees TV programme called Make Me Laugh. It was a cold, wet day at the Royal Lancaster Hotel in London, just up the road from Marble Arch. Nervous doesn't describe how I felt! There were many comics, some well-known ones from the top club circuits and television including Duncan Norvelle, Duggie Small, Clive Webb, Alan J Bartley, Kenny Smiles, Andrew 'O' Connor, Adrian Walsh, Peter Piper, MickMiller, Dave Ismay, Larry Larkin and many more funny guys.

The audition was short and sweet, and only lasted about a minute or so. In fact it was just like my audition for the summer season in Jersey three years earlier. Wearing my pink UV suit (now dried out!) and carrying my exploding guitar I certainly made an entrance that they were sure not to miss!

I think everybody heard the exploding guitar as far afield as Oxford Street! If I did that today I would certainly be surrounded by the Police within seconds!

On a positive note, it caught the production team's attention, everybody's attention in fact, and I didn't get a chance to do much else….I was in! Another special night, or was it daytime, I can't remember.

When I found out that I was going to be on telly for the first time I cannot tell you how excited it made me feel. It would hopefully be a big feather in my cap and help further my career.

It was several weeks later when we flew from Luton Airport to the North East with Bernie Winters, the host for the series, for the filming of what was to be five programmes. Not one but five weeks on the telly….marvellous!

The format for the programme was that a member of the studio audience would be sitting in a chair out front and Bernie Chuchy Face Winters would have a quick welcome chat with them. Then three comedy acts, one at a time, would come out and have to make them laugh within sixty seconds.

The name of the game in truth was to NOT make them laugh too quickly as the more airtime you could get the better. Obviously, each member of the audience had their own sense of humour and hopefully they would eventually laugh within the minute. They tried hard not to laugh though as that was the idea!

There was a celebrity guest on the programme each week and Paul Shane, of Hi-De-Hi fame, was our celebrity. To his credit, like the true pro he was, he waited and waited and laughed just at the right moment to give us our time to shine. God bless him.

"First rule of comedy Spike……." I loved Hi-De-Hi which was filmed just down the road from Ipswich in Dovercourt Bay in Essex, near Harwich.

My fellow performers on that first programme were stand-up comedian, Nicky Martin and ventriloquist, Johnny Roberts who were both very funny guys. Nearly all of my comedy was visual. I hoped that the person in the chair would crack at the stupid props and my off the wall ideas, more so than just stand-up.

Obviously, to start with I had the exploding guitar and I made that last for about ten seconds. The whole studio audience fell about laughing, I think it was laughter, probably a few of them were in shock, it was a very loud bang! The guy in the chair nearly had a heart attack!

Here are some of the visual gags I did with props;

Prince Charles with giant foam ears holding the baby Wills, "Have you seen my little Willy?"

Dame Edna in her over the top glasses, "Hello possums, I'm as happy as a pig in ch.....chiffon. I said to my husband Norm, "Why don't you kiss me like you used to?" He gets out of bed and I said, "Where are you going?" He said, "To get my teeth?"

Wearing a massive foam cowboy hat.....John Wayne

Riding a hobby horse with clothes on it......Clothes horse!!

One legged horse.........Clop!

Throw the gun........Gunslinger!

A cowboy wearing brown paper shoes, brown paper clothes, brown paper hat..........he was a Rustler!

A cornflake box on my head with the mouth and eyes cut out.... "Why can't I have proper glasses like the other kids dad?"

Tommy Cooper carrying a box of tissues. I throw them out one at a time....a tissue, a tissue...all fall down (throw them all out!)

A cardboard skeleton......Slimmer of the Year! With a lampshade on the skeleton.......a shade heavier!

As the Swedish Chef from The Muppet Show I showed dinner plates to the audience, two or three china plates I rattle first then throw three or four paper ones out into the audience!

This was all very silly and childlike in places but that was the idea back then, it was over thirty years ago! Subtlety and cleverness went out of the window.

It wasn't supposed to be Mock the Week or Live from the Apollo or even Britain's Got Talent. Most of the comedy I used on that very first TV programme was just for that particular format and nothing more.

It seems very basic looking back on it now. The material I used on Make Me Laugh was ok at the time and served a purpose and what's more it led to further TV exposure for me!

Chapter Sixteen

My Gig with Lee

I wanted to buy a really smart outfit for stage and ditch the flashy coloured suits I'd been wearing to date.

So a friend of mine put me in contact with a reputable tailor, Borovicks in Berwick Street, Soho, London. I picked out the material in an ivory colour and it was just what I wanted. Suits you Sir! They said they would send it in the post and I paid up front - what a knob! A few weeks later the suit came in the post, wrapped in a brown paper parcel. I unwrapped it and it had more creases than a pleated skirt!

My wife Pauline couldn't control herself and fell about laughing. I found it difficult to see the funny side and I had to bin it. I should have gone back to the tailors and told them to shove it where the sun don't shine. That might have got the creases out!

Can I see your cheapest suit? He gave me a mirror!

Do you know what would go well with that suit Sir? A bloody good iron!

Quasimodo said to the tailor, "Have you got a suit to fit me?" The Tailor replied, "If we have, someone's got the sack!"

Two months later and still fuming about my coat of many creases, I entered one of the heats for the Middlesex and Herts. Country Club Search for a Star competition. It was quite a prestigious talent event at the time and many acts took part, some with vast talent and experience.

I thought I had done my best fifteen minutes and won the heat and then went on to win the final. The prize was a cheque for £500. Oh to be a professional!

From the dizzy heights of winning a provincial talent contest to the rent a crowd at Rosie O'Gradys Holiday Park in Clacton. I have learnt over the years that you have to wear many hats. The more varied the material and changing my act accordingly meant that I had a better chance of success.

From a theatre support to a late night holiday centre, a hostile stag night or army base to a TV show. They are vastly different audiences and atmospheres, all with their own different tastes and comedy preferences. The smaller private holiday parks could be great fun being more intimate, but the larger family rooms could be a lot harder because of the atmosphere. There would be children in the audiences sometimes so once again, visual comedy was the main format:

Holding Orville the puppet, "I wish I could fly right up to the sky, but I can't. You can".......and I'd kick him into the audience!

Benny from Crossroads, "I do read that 95% of all road accidents do happen within three miles of home, so I moved!"

John Wayne wearing a massive foam cowboy hat and walking around the audience and when back on stage, "I just got off the stage."
Silly, but it got a laugh!

Bird impressions
A robin....pinch a drink from a table!

A puffin.....breathe heavily!

A lark....don't do that!

A wild duck.....get off my frigging pond!

A chicken walking backwards.....doodle doodle cock!

It was all very basic and very visual, nothing too clever either, and of course the exploding guitar! That shut the kids up. Sometimes it woke them up and mummy wasn't happy! A crying baby and another nappy!

I did look forward to returning to the regular establishments which included; Woodhall Country Club and the Clock Restaurant on the A1 at Welwyn, the Embassy Suite in Colchester, Beach Station at Felixstowe, the Silver Skillet at Maidenhead and a wonderful little social club at Whittlesford near Cambridge. I so enjoyed these feel good venues, mind you there were some that were tougher than others, but hey, playing safe is easy. I do enjoy a challenge and I have had my fair share of those. I once did an Animal Rights Barbeque!

I always thought the smaller cabaret establishments were a taster for the bigger ones. Experience is everything, as I keep saying.......

Later on that year I went to Saxavord in the Shetlands. This was the beginning of a run of engagements for CSE, Combined Services Entertainments.

It was such a change from the norm, a variety show where they flew all the acts out to perform for a small group of squaddies. They were great fun and tip top shows.

I was in the Army for only one day. The Sergeant Major said at the end of the day, "I didn't see you in Camouflage class?" I said, "Thanks very much!"

The year ended with Christmas runs at the Barking Fox which was very close to home and then office parties at the Osterley Comfort Inn on the A4. Office parties consisted of lots of young people and three words you don't want to hear...
....a free bar!

One and all were partying away and there I was hoping that they would give me a chance. What a job, but they usually did and the drive home became a better one. There was no M25 at the time though we had that pleasure to come!

The work continued to roll in and they were busy times for me the eighties. My act was building and improving consistently and the regular bread and butter gigs were helping with this with a special every so often. The year started off really well and end with my second telly. No, I didn't buy another one!

It was around this time that I performed a show with the now mega famous, mega funny, Lee Evans. It is 1984, over thirty years ago, and he was by no means a household name then but you could see he was soon going to be. The night in question was an ITV Telethon Charity and I remember it for one reason in particular. It was filmed at the Riverside Theatre in Woodbridge, near Ipswich and Lee was doing his standup routine when he suddenly lay down on the stage, but as he did so, he caught the upright microphone stand and it fell full pelt right onto his face! It was one of those heavy pump action stands and it must have hurt him, blood was spurting from his nose. Of course the audience cracked up, as you do, they thought it was part of his act but to his credit Lee carried on regardless and finished his set. What a pro! I would love to have the chance to meet up with him after all this time to see if he remembers the incident. What a career he has had, and for me they don't come much funnier.

A run of nights at Northrepps Country Club on the North Norfolk coast was next with comedian Ray Randall and a Touch of Class, a tip top Production Company. Ray was a very droll, deadpan comic from the North East, he was a funny looking guy but unfortunately I watched him struggle a few times. He was so laid back when sometimes the audiences needing attacking. I don't mean with a knife or suchlike, but to just get at them and up the pace a bit.

I then returned to Baileys at Watford to support the Drifters. What a fantastic group and they filled the room every night, the atmosphere was electric and I loved it. I then supported The Three Degrees at the Night Out in Birmingham, which was another sell out week, probably because they were on the bill! Ha ha! In between these weeks I would quickly have my feet placed firmly back on the ground working at York Hall, Bethnall Green, Highpoint Prison in Suffolk and East Tilbury Working Men's Club in Essex. What a great leveller this show business was turning out to be yet again.

East Tilbury WMC took no prisoners and did not pussy foot around. Subtlety once again went out of the window. It was very rough to say the least. The most fulfilling part of the evening was finding my car was still there after the gig!

I was parking my car and a voice said, "Twenty quid to look after your car mate?" I said, "I'll be ok Officer!"

I said, "I've got a Rottweiler on the back seat." He replied, "Does it put out fires?"

Two girls were in the cinema and one said, "The bloke beside me is playing with himself!" Her friend said, "Take no notice." She replied, "I can't, he's using my hand!"

A girl took me back to her place and she took off her wig and put it in the drawer, then put her glass eye in the drawer, false teeth, false boobs, and her wooden leg, all in the drawer. She said: "Come to bed?" I said, "I'll have more fun in the drawer! I'm going now, I think I left it in my other pants!"

In Essex, everybody's friend is called, Tosser!

In Tilbury the population stays the same. When a sixteen year old girl gets pregnant, the father buggers off!

She had seven kids, all boys, all called Tyrone. When asked, "how do you tell them apart?" She replied, "By their surname!"

The more up market, quality work was starting to flow in now on a more regular basis. A Gene Pitney tour took me to some really nice theatres including; Nottingham Royal Centre, Northampton Derngate, Croydon Fairfield Halls, St. David's Hall in Cardiff, the Floral Pavillion in New Brighton, Ferneham Hall in Fareham and Lincoln, Harrogate, Oldham, Basildon, St. Albans to name just a few. Gene had a wonderful following and the venues were always full. What a lovely man and a great artist he was.

The travelling was becoming a way of life, but home life was also fantastic and the kids were growing up fast. They were getting used to daddy being away now and again.

What does your daddy do? He's a Gypsy!

Travelling is always a bit more bearable when you know there is a really good gig lying in wait. The Pitney tour was followed by yet more favourable gigs. Two trips for Combined Services Entertainment, a four dayer on Benbecula in the Outer Hebrides and another in Northern Ireland. Being in the latter could be somewhat tricky. One time we had to break off in the middle of the show as the troops were called out!

Irish gags are somewhat antiquated now in the modern era, not because they are racist, but they are just not en vogue anymore. I would then, and do now, turn an Irish based joke into something else.......

The rather stupid acid bath murderer lost his arm by pulling the plug out!

The apprentice electrician; blue to red, blue to green, blue to bits!

The husband said to his wife, "Haven't you got little titties?" She said, "Get off my back will ya!"

No mention of an Irishman anywhere.....

78

When I came back I accompanied the loveable Jimmy Jones on his first theatre tour together with another great support act, the wonderful Linda Nolan. We had a fabulous tour playing yet again to full houses each night. As I said, Jimmy was one of those kind and humble comics. Not only would he ask you NOT to leave stuff out that was getting big belly laughs, he would give me lines and help me improve my craft and technique where he felt I needed it!

Jim Davidson was the same, not afraid to follow someone who was getting good laughs, trying to make their way up in the business.

Sadly, not all comedy top of the bill acts are like that. It does seem very insecure. I relish the challenge of following performers who have done really well. The last thing I want is follow an act who has died on their arse! High standards and competition makes you work harder and get better – have no fear. So the first half of the year was a ball with top quality venues and artistes. Gigs were flowing and I was beginning to think that I had some Romany blood in me after all!

The Watneys Roadshows were in full swing, then along came The Talk of the East, a fine nightclub in Norwich, The Embassy Theatre in Skegness, The White Rock in Hastings with the Barron Knights, and three nights at The Sparrows Nest theatre in Lowestoft with Vince Hill and Norman Collier! There were lots of Essex and East Coast holiday parks and another week at Baileys in Watford.

A trip to the Hook of Holland from Harwich on the Stenna Line seemed like a good idea. Going over, everybody was sober and the first show was no problem. Coming back however, thanks to the duty free, the audience were slightly drunk well pissed to be honest! It was a completely different atmosphere…..

Two blokes were at the Bar and one said, "Your round?" The other said, "So are you, you fat bastard!"

A fella asked for a pint of beer and the bloke behind the Bar said, "One pence." He then asked for a whiskey, "Two pence." Then a cigar, "Five pence." The fella says, "Cheap prices Landlord?" He replied, "I'm not the Landlord, he's upstairs doing to my missus what I'm doing to his business!"

A bloke was laid flat out on the floor against the Bar. I said to the Barman, "He's had a few?" He said, "No, just the one." I said, "Bloody hell, can I have what he's just had?" And the Barman smacked me in the face!

A man won the jackpot on the one-armed bandit and was paid out in ten pence pieces! He went home drunk and when trying to find his front door key drops the coins everywhere. He opens the front door in the morning and finds one hundred and fifty pints of milk on the doorstep!

Back to Victorias on the A20, the Osterly Inn on the A4 and the Clock Restaurant on the A1 for more Christmas parties and the year was complete, well almost. There was another special, my second TV appearance on 3:2:1 with Ted Rogers. It was a very popular programme watched by millions each week but it didn't quite turn out as we would have liked. Dusty Bin......where are ya?!

Young Zany ... Who's a pretty boy then!

Me and my sister Jan -
"Blond Bombshells"

Rushmere Hall
Junior School,
me with the ball

me bottom left.

Musical Comedy Double Act

★SPLIT PERSONALITY★

MICK LANDER   Ipswich 43451
STEVE SPINKS   Ipswich 218416

G.E.H. & Achilles Football Clubs
invite you to a

New Year Dance
with
Terry & George plus *Split Personality*

Friday 13th January 1978, 8.00 to 12.00pm

Manor Ballroom
St. Margarets Green

Bar Extension
Ticket £1

Me with the Kevin Keegan ...
just like that!

Blackpool Pontins Talent Final 1978,
with the great Emlyn Hughes.

All the gang from the 1980 Jersey Travelling Show
including John Clown, (aka Walker).

Talent Show Final at Pontins, Hemsby, June 1978.

Early 80's

Sunday morning League Champions - me with the ball, again!

My very good friends, Ann and John Booth,
holding baby James with Uncle Reg.

Me at a local Boxing Charity event with the very funny Billy Dainty.

Me with my manager Barry,
alongside Paul Shane
& Faith Brown.

Off to the North East,
from Luton Airport to record
'Make Me Laugh' with funny
man Bernie Winters.

Setting the props for
'Make Me Laugh'.

My celebrity guest on 'Make Me Laugh',
Paul Shane.

90

The Platters with Herb Reid at
Goldiggers, Chippenham

1983, me as Worzel Gummidge

1984, 3-2-1 with Ted Rogers

Me in 1984 with
the legendary Jimmy Jones
on his first theatre tour

The exploding guitar on 3-2-1

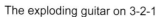

91

Funny man Norman Collier at
Sparrow's Nest, Lowestoft, 1984

Sparrow's Nest, Lowestoft with
Vince Hill, 1984

Skegness 1985, Butlins
with Alan Randall,
the George Fornby impersonator

On tour with Gene Pitney

The Three Degrees,
at the 'Night Out'
in Birmingham

Bailey's Nightclub at Watford with
Les Dennis and Dustin Gee

Bailey's Nightclub, Watford
with the Drifters

Bailey's at Watford
with the Commodores

Me and my cousin Stevie - 2015
(we had no photos of us back in the late 70's!)

In the studio recording the Christmas single, 'Carol Singing Startime'

With Claire & James
Sydney Harbour
Bridge 2004

Darling Harbour,
Sydney, 2004
with Claire & James

Chapter Seventeen

Dusty Bin

I was sharing the bill with Brendon Shine, a well-known Irish singer and the Minting Sisters, a lovely vocal harmony girl group. All seemed well, I thought. I opened up with the exploding guitar. There was a big response from the studio audience and then the Stage Manager said that we had to do it again as the Bass player in the orchestra wasn't mic'd up. To this day I can't understand who would have given a toss! I'm about to blow up a guitar, any fine tuning goes out of the window, surely?

Anyway, the second time the response was somewhat muted. Surely on reflection couldn't they have used the reaction from the first time around? Unfortunately, at the end of the day I was left in the hands of the editing team.

My mate Shane Richie also recorded 3:2:1 and he wasn't over the moon either with the outcome and if we ever got above ourselves we'd both say, just watch 3:2:1 and that will bring you back down to earth with a bump! Maybe I'm being a bit harsh here as the rest of the act did go well.

I have a brother – he's an only child!

My brother had one aim in life and missed!

Very lazy my brother, he married a pregnant women – how lazy is that?!

I then went into my Worzel Gummidge routine where I stayed in costume to give the contestant the clues that they had to decipher. I could never work out those bloody clues!

From Yorkshire Television I then went into the BBC Studios in Norwich and recorded a Christmas single, on vinyl 45 rpm, and it was called Carol Singing Startime, the music was by a good friend of mine from Ipswich, George Baker, and I wrote the lyrics and did the impressions.

The BBC programme was called Squeezebox and was presented by local personality and entertainer, Pete Sayers. The record was great fun and I keep saying that I should update it and perform it today. The chorus, or hook I think they call it, is very catchy!

Although 3 2 1 was not my finest hour by any means, not everything you do in life is going to turn out exactly how you want it to. There will always be minor setbacks and trust me there were a few more to come. The most important thing for me is how to get through these setbacks and turn a negative into a positive.

For me personally, any setbacks make me even stronger and more determined to work harder and get better.....and improve in every way possible.

It had now been five years for me as a professional funny guy, work was flourishing with a variety of venues and audiences right across the board.

This business is so varied and long may it continue. It makes it so much more stimulating and satisfying knowing you have to keep changing and improving all the time. You know what they say – familiarity breeds contempt.

Kings at Canvey Island became a regular late night hotspot. The Essex nightclub had Triple Cream performing, a fabulous backing band and nowadays a superb comedy show band in their own right, and the inimitable compere, the manic Johnny Clark. He has calmed down a bit but there was a great atmosphere at Kings where everyone could let off steam! It would be very late when I went on stage and there was no time to be laid back. I had to get them quick and keep the buggers – great nights!

I had another week at Baileys with the fabulous Dr. Hook, then a slice of good fortune came my way!

Tony, the Gaffer at Victorias Nightclub in Kent, knew George Savva who was the governor at Blazer's Nightclub in Windsor. He had a word and the next thing I knew I was supporting Ken Dodd there. It was an exceptional night. There were nine hundred people in the audience, all employees of the Water board!

Obviously, with Doddy topping the bill, you are guaranteed a proper comedy audience. By jove, what a lovely day! It was at the time when Ken had just won his tax evasion court case.

We are the Diddle Men......!

He had to have open heart surgery and they found another ten grand!

"Did you know that Ken Dodd's dad's dog's died?" "Did he?" "No, Doddy!"

Ken is renowned for being on stage for hours, literally. He never stops – it's his trademark. They reckon if he'd been found guilty and he got five years in jail, he would have done ten!

98

Anyway, after my spot, George was more than happy and consequently gave me more dates at Blazers supporting Gerard Kenny and Kool and The Gang.

A Captain's Day cabaret at my own Golf Club at Rushmere in Ipswich, was followed by yet another week at Baileys with The Commodores. They were one of my favourite groups at that time and I watched them every night. It was fantastic!

Every time I worked at Baileys it was always packed. They had great top of the bills and it was wonderful exposure for me. Lots of work was to come from working at this vibrant nightclub.

I was now doing the Butlins circuit on a regular basis in the summer, every Thursday and Friday at Skegness and then weekends at Pwllheli and Minehead. There would be a lot of travelling once again and I used to break down on more than one occasion, not me, the car, so it was important to belong to a breakdown service company.

My brakes went once, I was going down a hill and I just managed to avoid crashing. The man from the AA turned up, don't know why, I don't even drink!

He looked under the bonnet and said, "You've lost some fluid." I said, "You're bloody right I've lost some fluid!!"

"Are you in the Relay?" I said, "Why, have I got to run home?!"

In June of 1985 Butlins were celebrating their fiftieth anniversary at Skegness. One night when I was on stage all the power went! Alan Randall, the great George Formby impersonator, who was on the bill, came on to the stage with a torch and a broom and started to clean-up. It was such a funny moment, you had to be there!

A phone call out of the blue came from Billy Cocker Forrest asking me if I would like to go back to Jersey to do an end of season two weeks at the Sunshine Hotel, sharing the bill with one of my all-time favourite funny men, Mick Miller. The Sunshine was a small, intimate room with a great atmosphere and I jumped at it. This was to be the start of a long lasting love affair with the island working in summer seasons for the next seven years!

Chapter Eighteen

New Faces

After a gig at a very nice private Christmas party at the Spider's Web Hotel in Watford, I came out to the car park and my car was not there! It had been stolen, my treasured XR3i Ford Escort, apparently by Travellers. I called them something else! The car was found six weeks later in a field somewhere, completely burnt out and written off! Maybe they'd seen the act!

I am so glad that the gig had gone well, the governor who had booked me for the function paid for a cab for me to get back home to Ipswich. The fare was £100, a lot of money in those days. My dad was with me that night as he loved to see me work and he was furious at first. He was swearing profusely but after I told him about the £100 and the cab home he calmed down. Bless him, he was such a worrier, with nothing to worry about!

What a lovely gesture, although in return I went back on stage and did another twenty minutes whilst I was waiting for the taxi! There is no such thing as a free lunch – or dinner!

The work was still coming in thick and fast, more regular cabaret restaurants were being added all the time, including La Taverna at Epping and the Downtown Restaurant at Rotherhythe, many a great night was had at these busy venues – a meal, dancing, cabaret and late night drinking! How sad is it that most of these great cabaret and nightclub venues have been closed or knocked down now.

It was around this time that I would be sharing the bill with my buddy Shane Richie and the likes of Bradley Walsh, Joe Pasquale and Bobby Davro amongst others. They would all be on the scene then and have now gone on to bigger and better things. They are all funny guys and I am proud of them.

The Hens and Stag nights were still rife, as well as the social clubs and holiday centres, the bread and butter gigs as I like to call them. The material had to be suitable for those down to earth venues.

I said to the wife, "Do you fancy a little bit of hanky panky?" She said, "you've had that!" Do you know, I couldn't remember!

She said, "You're taking your time." I replied, "I can't think of anybody!"

She said, "I want you to tie me to the bed." So I did, and she said, "Now you can do what you like." So I had a shave and went down the pub!

Also, as in previous years, there were once again some specials and this year was to be no exception.

Having enjoyed success with Mick Miller at the Sunshine Hotel, I was asked to go back to Jersey and do a full season at the Chateau Plasir on the Five Mile Road at St. Ouen. I was to star with Shane for six weeks, whereafter, he would go on to Bournemouth and complete the summer season there and have fun with The Nolans, well one of them anyway!

The two of us put together a double act, around thirty minutes or so, but also performed our own slots as well. We had a ball in those six weeks and later took the double act on to several gigs and better still, a tour of the Falkland Islands six months later for Combined Services Entertainment.

Anyway, I digress, more about the Falklands later......

The show at the Chateau in Jersey starred a cracking Elvis like singer called Toni Morrel and Jack Young, a trumpeter and singer supreme. His brother Robert came to replace Shane and it was a very happy season. The venue was not considered to be one of the most prestigious on Jersey but it was a very down to earth club atmosphere and the show went extremely well.

The audiences came from all over the island, the UK and France and the climate, the people and the work was second to none. What was even better was that my family would come over and the kids loved it!

I was hoping at the time that this would be a stepping stone for bigger and more prestigious seasons to come. Robert Young was, and hopefully still is, a fabulous tenor. He had a wicked sense of humour and he liked a drink or two. I remember that season was indeed great fun with a great company.

Looking back now my act was still very raw. I was naturally funny but a long way short of where I wanted it to be especially with the content. People said that I had my own style of working but I felt that there was still a lot to improve on.

Gags relating to Jersey were starting to emerge and my routines would grow and grow holding me in good stead for the coming seasons ahead. Jersey is a very small island, an area of approximately nine by five miles.

I was driving along the A1. The A1, it's like a pavement over here!

I came to a small clearing. It was the A12!

Two Bulls in a field and one said, "Bit chilly out here, think I'll nip in that shed and slip into another Jersey!"

There was still a lot of visual content and props in the act, most of which over the years I have stopped using. Slowly, stand-up material would become the main part of my act. More clever, observational, topical comedy replaced old worn out and well used jokes. I had to be edgier and nearer the knuckle when needed.

Working with Shane, or Reg as we often called each other, was a delight. The double act, Reg and Reg was a refreshing change. There was an instant rapport and chemistry between us and we had lots of fun with much ad-libbing that became infectious, bouncing off each other. The audience loved it.

I would walk out first to introduce the act, then Reg would appear from the back of the room. "Micky, someone has left their lights on in the car park." I would say: "Get the number," and after a few minutes he would walk back in with the bumper (or rather a prop bumper) with the number plate attached. It was a massive laugh!

We would sing The Eye of The Tiger, the Rocky theme tune, then end up singing the last line as, off we go to a disco. Then into the Birdie Song, daft and silly, but very funny, we liked it!

Then came the funniest part of all, we performed a parody of the Paul Anka hit Diana. Shane was Lady Di and I was Prince Charles with the cap and big ears! It brought the house down! Living Doll, the Cliff Richard and The Young Ones version was also a big hit for us, it was very visual as you can imagine. We wrote a bank robber sketch about two bank robbers named Reg and Reg who were sitting in a car waiting to rob a bank. The sketch included lots of funny lines and plenty of ad-libs. We closed our set with That's What Friends Are For and a great time was had by all. They were happy days.

My own set was littered with gags and silly off the wall situations plus many impressions, including my hero, the great Norman Wisdom and the exploding guitar was always a good opener!

My Quasimodo routine was taking shape, or rather not, if you get my drift! There were only so many gags with The Hunchback of Notre Dame and I was searching high and low to add parodies to the character. I did spoofs on; Dead Ringer for Love, Up on the Roof and Wake me up before you Go Go. Quasi was later to be aired on another TV Special.

The Monday Club, which was a weekly afternoon variety show, was in full swing raising money for the Jersey Variety Club and it was also an opportunity to meet many of the performers who were working on the Island. I used this time to go on stage and do my bit by trying out new material and improvise or improv as it is more commonly known today. Many of my ideas and routines came from trying them out on a Monday afternoon at those charity lunches. I would also get a chance to see some of the quality acts do a small cameo. I always enjoy watching other entertainers doing their stuff.

You can learn a lot from other performers but not by taking their material! Where is the satisfaction in that, especially if you want to further your career and be your own person with your own identity?

Another opportunity for TV work was being asked to play Jimmy Savile in an episode of Jim'll Fix It. At the time this was a good job for me and a real coup, and was obviously years before the Yewtree Investigation and we found out what we now know about Savile.

The story goes that a girl (we can call her Shirley) wanted to meet John Nettles of TV's Bergerac fame. Bergerac was a very big hit for the BBC and was filmed entirely on location in Jersey and was immensely popular.

He was an extremely clever cop our Bergerac, he could solve the crime every week in just forty-five minutes! My job was to don a track suit, blond wig, large cigar and with my accomplice Bob, a local bodybuilder from Jersey, con the holiday makers out of donations on the seafront along Gorey Harbour. We would collect money from the unsuspecting punters and get away with the bucket full of cash, all in a good cause of course!

As the plot went, Shirley sees this deception and she then contacts PC Plod, Mr Bergerac who turns up before our getaway.

That was fairly simple but the story ended when I got pushed into the harbour by the young Shirley, followed swiftly by John Nettles! My family, who were over at the time and the crowd of onlookers found this highly amusing.

Unfortunately, I am not a strong swimmer, in fact I am aqua-phobic, is there such a word?

At the time I had this Kevin Keegan perm and the make-up department had tied my hair in bunches to hold the wig on, but when I hit the water about twenty five feet below I hasten to add, the wig came off and I was splashing about like an epileptic alligator and fighting for breath!

They said it made good telly, charming! I have learnt to swim properly now and the perm has gone as well....... along with some of my hair!

I've had a sun roof put in!

I've got wavy hair. I'm waving it goodbye!

I'm using that new shampoo now, wash and come back!

I got this cheap wig. It's got a hole in it!

There are many venues where you can be sure of a warm, friendly atmosphere but the pressure was on more when I worked the late night cabaret circuit such as La Taverna in Epping, Victorias in Kent, Newmarket Cabaret Club and others. The crowd would be somewhat boisterous, noisy and over the top and I would be expected to handle these difficult situations. Failure or a struggle to win them over on a regular basis would and could mean no more work at these venues. News spreads fast in this business, especially the bad news.

Luckily it made me more determined to have the confidence and content for every situation whether I was laid back to an upmarket audience and being spotlessly clean or where I had to mix it and go in stronger and be more risqué. It was also important for me to gauge an audience as quickly as possible, preferably within the first few minutes or so.

Another one off was the Southern Area Entertainer of the Year at the Kings nightclub on the beautiful island of Canvey! My very good friend, Johnny Clark hosted the venue and said to me, "You'll piss it," a well-known showbizzy term for, you're a very funny boy and you've got a very good chance of winning this! Keep it clean was the advice on the night as the judges were well known in certain circles and television opportunities were beckoning or so I was lead to believe.

To cut a long story short I did not win. My clean and clever routines were cast aside for the more risqué Blackpool comic Buddy Lee. There is being cheeky, spicy and saucy but Buddy was somewhat blue and the audience loved it, he went on late so he played to them. A very funny guy though! You can't win them all, sometimes you nail it, sometimes not. I played it safe that time and it wasn't to be. Putting it in contrast with New Faces there was no contest.

This year was turning out to be quite special, peppered with the usual gigs. The Clock at Welwyn, The Downtown Restaurant at Rotherhythe, the Osterley Comfort Inn and a very posh New Year's Eve do at the Great Danes Hotel in Hollingbourne, Kent. The luvvies were all dressed up in tuxedos and ball gowns and there was I with my squeaky clean material! It seemed that every type of audience had been put in front of me throughout that year and a wealth of different material and approach was certainly a key factor of my success and continuing work, versatility comes to mind. Every now and again I was faced with a staring competition but for me that beats a noisy rabble any day. In today's world, when you are a name people come and see You and they know what to expect. When they don't know you and you go into their pond sometimes you have to work that little bit harder.

There was so much in the mix; TV, theatre, talent shows, nightclubs, social clubs, holiday centres, army bases and Stag and Hen Nights. Also, there were so many agents with their own venues on their own patches. Most of them have all gone now I'm sorry to say, maybe one or two are still remaining but will probably still be paying the same fee as all those years ago!

As it turned out the bread and butter gigs were moving along very nicely thank you and I was making a decent living. There was the odd special which, apart from being a refreshing change, gave me that little extra lift in confidence and I knew that if I kept plugging away the rewards would come.

Just before the season ended at the Chateau, I had the chance to do another special. I had auditioned way back in January at the Beach Station Caravan Park in Felixstowe, Suffolk and it was for New Faces, TV's biggest talent show at the time. Richard Holloway, the Producer, was there along with several other artistes and the general public.

All the acts were chomping at the bit, the reward being a major TV Talent Show watched by millions. Although the acts wanted to do well in front of the general public the more important issue was to impress the TV Producer and to present an act suitable for the telly.

I was now performing Diana, the Paul Anka song on my own. It was a real crowd pleaser doing it with Shane, aka Reg, he with the blue ladies hat and me with the ears! It was even funnier now with me wearing each hat, one for the Lady Di line of the song and vice versa with Prince Charles. Towards the end of the song I'd get the hats and voices mixed up. It proved to be a strong ending to the audition and Mr. Holloway was suitably impressed and I got through to the programme.

I flew from Jersey to Birmingham, recorded the programme and flew back to finish off the season. Cocker Forrest, who was my original agent for Jersey in 1980, was not overly pleased with me taking two nights off but he couldn't really say no to a prime time television appearance? Have a day off Billy, I'm on the telly!

New Faces had been going for a while and it had been ten years earlier that Jim Davidson and Lenny Henry first found fame on the programme. The show was recorded at the Hippodrome in Birmingham with Marti Caine, a wonderful host and comedienne.

There were some talented acts on the bill that week; Maggie Dee - a Scottish singer, Adam Quest - a singer from the Midlands, a group called Made in Japan, Brett Sherwood and Lesley Ann - a magic act, another comic who I knew well called Paul James and yours truly.

Maggie won the viewer's vote – allegedly! Don't be bitchy I hear you say! I also recall that during the rehearsals the local singer, Adam, gave us all a little gift, a keepsake lucky charm, whatever you want to call it. Anyway, he won the audience vote, fancy that! Double bitchy moment!

The programme aired two weeks later on the 3rd of October 1986 and I was more than pleased with my set. Vince Hill and Nina Myskow liked what I did. Yes, Nina liked me! I did the Diana parody and a Chinese restaurant routine. Unfortunately, the third judge, Simon Napier Bell, the then Manager of Wham didn't particularly find me funny. What does he know about comedy anyway? Wham... I'm Your Man, well not in this case!

That night when millions were watching New Faces, I was performing at Edmonton Trades and Labour Club, North London. Well, I was there in body but my mind was elsewhere! Two days later I was supposed to be at Hillingdon Social Club, West London. It got cancelled the day before due to the fact that comedy wasn't working at the club. No word of a lie, maybe Simon Napier Bell was on the Committee!

Chapter Nineteen

We're In the Army Now

I could never see myself as a Soldier. I'm a lover not a fighter.

I went into the Army and Navy Surplus Store and asked, "Have you got any camouflage jackets?" He said, "Yeah, but we can't find them!"

When I tell people that I went to the Falklands they are impressed at first but when I say it was five years after the conflict their interest wanes somewhat, but it was still a great thrill for me.

On reflection it was another major point in my career, not too many people can say they spent two weeks in the Malvinas entertaining the locals as well as the troops.

It was a great start to the year and this was a trip never to be forgotten, or repeated.

I had a once in a lifetime experience.........never again!

The tour was delayed a day due to prevailing weather conditions, it was the middle of winter and extremely cold weather. A very talented show company had been put together. My buddy Shane, a comedy magician called Simon Lovell, Lizanne - a singer and saxophonist, four dancers, a backing duo Graham and Chris aka Pea Green Philharmonic Pullover Set, and yours truly. It turned out to be a highly successful tour and an adventure which will live on forever in my memory.

Flying out of Brize Norton, Oxfordshire that cold evening in January on a tristar plane with nearly three hundred passengers to the Acension Islands was something I wasn't looking forward to. I hate flying at the best of times! Mind you it could have been worse, we could have been flying SleasyJet or Ruin Air!

They show you where the exits are, why? If we crash there will be hundreds!

In case of an emergency, put your head between your legs. If I could do that I wouldn't leave the house!

If we have to land on the sea... on the sea? If it can't fly how is it gonna float?!

They give you a whistle. I'd prefer an airport!

It was such a bumpy landing because of the wind and I said to Captain Kangaroo, "Did we land or were we shot down?!"

It wasn't long after that we had the Lockerbie disaster and any material about flying was obviously put on hold, for me anyway.

The outward eight hour flight was a calm one and there was no flatulence, sorry, turbulence! I got a chance to go and have a look around the cockpit which was a great opportunity.

I said to the Pilot, "Do your planes crash very often?" He replied, "No, just the once!"

We arrived at the Ascension Islands at 4.30 am, no time difference to the UK. It was in the mid-70s, very humid and such a contrast from back home. It was only a quick turnaround, about an hour and a half, and then we were on our way to Mount Pleasant in the Falkland Isles.

We touched down at 11.00 am and were now three hours behind the UK, so all in all we had two very long flights, plenty of food and drink but little sleep.

We left Mount Pleasant two hours later to fly out to our first outpost at Fox Bay. This time we travelled by Chinook helicopter which was very noisy and very cold. It felt like we were actually in the frigging army now, tied to the side of the chopper rather than in conventional seats!

Our first gig was well received and the audience consisted of locals who were nicknamed Bennys, and they gave us a standing ovation. (I can only think of Benny from Crossroads. I may be wrong.)

Shane and I would do most of the double act we did a few months earlier in Jersey, and our own sets as well. Silly visual stuff was going to win this audience over together with some earthy humour, localising a bit.

Fox Bay was basically a look-out post where soldiers would go out and check the terrain. The ninety or so personnel were mainly Scottish and consisted of the Argyles who were a great bunch of lads. I remember being told that the cost of keeping the outpost running was substantial and that the site was soon to be closed down.

We had an early start on day two and after taking photos of Fox Bay we headed by Bristow helicopter to our next venue, Mount Alice, which was two hundred and nineteen miles away from mainland Argentina. We arrived at Mount Alice in heavy cloud and the chopper was unable to land on the top of the hill so we had to travel by snow mobile to the outpost. This was brown trouser time for me!

A tour of Mount Alice was first on the agenda. It was a radar station set up to pick up enemy planes and it took only four months to build with a personnel of forty-eight!

The two hour show that night was great fun and the lads loved it. There was no swearing and no blue material, it wasn't needed or required. Pool and Bar football and a bit of drinking followed and by 1 a.m. we were all extremely knackered!

We were up again at 9.00am. on day three, packing once more for our next venture. The helicopter took all our gear first and then came back for us and the crew. Our next concert was at Byron Heights, a mountain site with a personnel of fifty and very similar to Mount Alice Radar Station, very windy and remote on the north of the Island. The show once again received a standing ovation, either that or all the audience decided to go for a pee at the same time! We had a good old sing song afterwards where the squaddies gave a great rendition of their funny wokka wokka song. It was a great night out with a great bunch of lads who had been starved of any entertainment for months on end.

It became the norm as once again we had an early start the following morning, a BV ride (all terrain vehicle) to the helicopter. It was very foggy and it felt like we were stuck in the middle of nowhere, oh we were...I forgot! It was a one hour helicopter ride to Mount Kent, our next outpost of call, and then another BV ride to the camp.

Trying to sleep in the afternoons was an option but with all the lads sharing one room it was difficult...I am a very light sleeper!

Mount Kent was another Radar Station with a personnel of fifty, there were no locals around at all, it was very barren, very windy and very foggy! Another brilliant show was again well received with the audience cheering, screaming and shouting their approval......thank God for alcohol!

There would be the odd wannabe heckler who liked to have a go, in a friendly way, mind you. They loved a little bit of banter!

Save your breath for blowing your girlfriend up!

I'm going to a party later. Do you want to come, they said bring your own dope!

Some people have a plant in the audience. I get a cabbage!

What do you use for a contraceptive, your personality?!

After the show the lads had a certain ritual which involved carrying each of us horizontally on their shoulders around the room which ended up with you hitting a large bell with your head! Shane hit the bell with great fervour and bravado but Simon took centre stage, needing stitches across his forehead! It was great fun and morale boosting, especially when it wasn't you who had been picked to do it!

We had an early start yet again and left our remote outpost and arrived at the Capital, Port Stanley on day five. This was the main location for troops and civilians.

It was a lot bigger than I first thought and over five hundred lads and a few lasses filled the floating barge. It was a much bigger venue than we had been used to and a video was being filmed at the same time.

When Shane and I sat on the huge stage we could see above us a motto which read; Whale Oil Beef Hooked, it was very funny.… (Read it again quickly!) We fell about before we had even started the act!

Instead of a hut we now had the luxury of staying at the 'Malvinas' Hotel, which was very comfortable. It felt five star after the last few days!

"Can we have breakfast in bed?" "Of course, can you bring your bed to the Canteen!"

The towels were lovely and fluffy, so soft that I couldn't shut my suitcase!

Nice hotel, not much passing trade though – we had a few Argie's come here a while ago, but they didn't stop long!

The show, now on video, still brings back great memories for me. Five hundred squaddies were packed into this great hall which I think was their gym. The show was received as you can guess with great appreciation, they went mad and showed it. A feeling myself and the gang will never forget.

The show format went like this: the dancers opened with a big production number and I would compere and do my slot. Lizanne then sang and played the saxophone followed by Simon doing his unique magic which was very clever and subtle. Shane would then do his show, which was be followed by our double act, more or less the same as Jersey. With us two anything could happen and it usually did. Ad libs were coming from everywhere including out front!

The audience loved the one liners and the visual and vocal comedy. They had all had a drink or two by now but no blue material was used, they didn't want it, but saucy and cheeky was ok. I did my comedy impressions, lots of voices from funny men past and present, several gags and some visual comedy. Quasimodo always went well, especially wearing a camouflage cloak!

A Soldier came home early one day and found the wife in bed with his best mate. He said, " Harry, I have to, but you?!"

He was in a Japanese Prisoner of War Camp. I said, "That must have been awful?" He replied, "It was, it rained every day!"

My granddad fought, but he still had to go!

On the morning before leaving Port Stanley we went to a lecture and watched a film of the conflict five years earlier and then went on a conducted tour of the battle areas. We travelled by Landrover to Tumbledown Mountain and saw the Argentinian positions in the mountains and where the British attacked them. It was all fascinating and a lot was learnt that day. A night off was welcomed and more importantly we had an early night before the trip back to Mount Pleasant the next day.

We were off on our travels again from the heady heights of Port Stanley to the very laid back Mount Pleasant Airport, our last stop of the Falklands tour. One hour by Landrover to the airport, nicknamed Death Star, or it was at the time! It was very big with all new units and single rooms. It was a bit like Milton Keynes, but we had a good night's sleep at last!

We had the afternoon off with a sound check at 5.00pm. and we were staying for three nights. The audiences consisted of Junior ranks, Sergeants and Officers with all shows getting their usual grand reception and success. The weather there could be very changeable, one minute sunny, then the next raining with gale force winds. Mind you there was a lot of snow back home at the time so we couldn't complain.

As everything was so new at Mount Pleasant Airport, the facilities were really good. There was a gymnasium, wet training facilities, squash courts, snooker tables and we even had time to relax! The concert that night was in the Sergeants Mess, they were very sociable and not quite as boisterous as the junior ranks.

It was now our last show of the tour and it wouldn't be long before our adventure would be coming to an end. Whilst Shane and I did radio interviews the rest of the gang went in a Hercules and saw rapier missiles. It was all a great adventure and all part of a days work!

We took the long flight back to the Ascension Isles and performed for the locals at their very small theatre in Georgetown. A small number of people living together in a close knit community offers up thought for the imagination. I can remember walking on stage in that small hut like theatre and there was a mother breastfeeding her baby boy on the front row! I remember being asked if I wanted a drink and I said, "I'll have what he's having – make it a double!" The strange thing was that the boy looked about five years old!

We were getting to understand why they were all called Benny's!

This remote part of the World, Georgetown, was obviously twinned with itself!

Father's Day is chaos and the family tree is a stump!

Before we left the Ascension Isles we went on a fishing trip and spent the rest of the day at the beach. The temperature was around 25 degrees centigrade and at 11.00 p.m. that night we went back to the beach to see the large Turtles laying their eggs which was fascinating. We had to keep very quiet and no photographs were allowed to be taken until all the eggs had been laid, apparently this was the law. The giant Turtle laid around two hundred eggs and only one or two will survive and hatch after six to eight weeks. Hark at me, sounding like a David Attenborough documentary.

On our last day I have this everlasting memory of Shane, or Reg as we were now called, (or Alfie Moon as some of you know him now), being considerably burnt by the sun, it was extremely hot on that last day. After a barbecue, a few beers and NO suntan lotion, Shane ended up having lips like Lesley Ash and both his eyelids almost stuck together. His eyes were almost closed up and he looked like an oriental Mick Jagger! It was a fun day and we all found it hilarious, not Shane of course. Luckily the shows were all done and dusted and the heat was off – not in Shane's case though!

So fifteen days away and it was back to blighty. What an adventure we had, an experience to treasure forever, never to be repeated.

Maybe some of you reading this may get an inkling into what it was like to be out there in the Falklands, albeit well after the War had ended. As they say, you had to be there!

My heart went out to those who lost their lives fighting for the cause. I'm not sure what cause, something called principal no doubt.

Their memory and bravado will live on forever.

Chapter Twenty

Falkland Isles to the Channel Isles

From the wonderful climate of the Ascension Islands to the cold snowy winter back home, and a gig at Canterbury Prison.

Trying to make inmates laugh can be punishing...ha ha! A lot of gigs are in Bars, in this case, behind bars! One inmate especially was having a go, between two roses there is always one prick, and he was reluctant to stop. The man in question was from a certain rough area. To try and shut him up I said, "Where you come from mate 75% of men make love in the shower. The other 25% are not in prison!" It was the biggest laugh of the night and it kept him quiet till he actually understood the joke and back he came again! It was a fun night in there but freedom is much better!

A mixture of shows lay ahead before a consecutive summer season back in Jersey. I did gigs at Achilles Football Club in Ipswich, who I used to play for, then Hunstanton, Wisbech, Ilford, Ford's at Dagenham and then a return to the prestigious East Tilbury Recreation Club!!

You don't often see sawdust on the floor anymore, very old fashioned. It was last night's furniture!

I was parking the car outside the club and I had to be careful not to park beside the burnt out cars! I don't remember how the show went as I was so worried about my car!

Living in Ipswich meant that the east coast holiday parks were in abundance and I spent years going up and down the A12 in both directions! I only wish they had road miles.....

In March 1987 I had a very strange experience. I was asked to do the Dover Harbour Board Social Club. There were two shifts and I did the first shift on one Friday and the second was the following Friday to a different audience. The first gig went really well and then......the Zeebrugge disaster happened. The Ferry involved was called the Herald of Free Enterprise and the doors had not been closed properly before departure and several lives were lost. It was a terrible disaster and I was surprised to be told that I was expected to go back and still do the second show.

114

I really did not want to go and what was worse, it was Friday the 13th! I have performed at many tough gigs over the years and they are not moments that you want to experience very often and this was one of them.

It was an awkward situation to be in but thankfully the show went ok.

The saying; the show must go on is sometimes used but in my mind the saying more applicable is….. Life goes on.

Now it was back to Jersey for me but this time not in a static show as last year but another travelling one similar to what I had experienced when turning pro back in 1980. This was better, a night off every week, better hotels and two holiday centres thrown in for good measure and comfort!

The circuit was for Modern Hotels. They had four hotels which were nice, friendly venues and it was a pleasure to work them.

The guv'nor was Paul Wagner, a Billy Connolly lookalike and soundalike! He produced, directed and managed the shows. Paul is a loveable, outgoing and hugely impressive character, he improved me in many ways and is still one of my best friends along with his lovely wife Kay. Waggy, as we affectionately called him, was inspirational. He would give constructive criticism such as, "You were shite!" and I would reply, "Aye Waggy, but it were good shite!"

Sometimes people pussyfoot around you. I am my own biggest critic, but Paul rated me and his wish was to see me improve and reach my full potential. He hasn't seen me perform for many years and I know he'd see a vast difference and improvement since those early years in Jersey. He'd still say, "You were shite." I love him!

He did me proud and after much persistence he arranged an audition for me at Caesars Palace in Jersey. He was constantly telling impresario Dick Ray to give me a chance to impress and it came just before the end of that season in 1987. Waggy was sure that I could make the step up and be a hit at this very prestigious venue.

The audition, or cameo as I like to call it, went really well and it was such a great feeling performing in the three hundred seater venue, it was a really intimate cabaret room with a touch of theatre to it. There were four acts, six dancers and a fabulous band.

I can remember hoping and wishing that Dick would be suitably impressed and I would get to work there. My wish came true, he liked what he saw and I was booked to do the following season. Consequently, I worked there for five years in a row!

I was moving in the right direction and the burning desire to do better was taking shape. Life was good and gigs were coming in thick and fast. The Modern Hotel circuit was so enjoyable. Being part of a successful show every night was very rewarding. We had Cetan Mani, whose real name was Jay from Liverpool, a knife thrower and fire-eater and a truly gifted speciality act. Then we had two sisters, Paula and Karen, named Sweet Illusion, and we all got on extremely well. It was a fun show and a fab season.

We opened the show with me and the girls singing I'm So Excited and Dancing on the Ceiling, then Sweet Illusion did their set. This was followed by Cetan Mani throwing knives at his attractive assistant, Adele, who became White Dove when on stage. I then closed the show with my exploding guitar routine followed by a My Way impression routine with comedy voices, a gaggle of gags, Diana and Quasimodo and then Norman Wisdom to finish. We had Rex and Billy who were a very experienced backing duo and we would close with a rock ' n' roll set with the girls.

Not only did we have the Monday charity lunches for the Variety Club of Jersey, we also did a Saturday club which was at lunchtime at the Metropole Hotel Side Bar, one of the Modern Hotels.

Yours truly would host a lunchtime gag session, a sort of open mic stand up slot whereby various comics or would be wannabes could come up and have a go at getting laughs.

The goalposts were somewhat widened on these occasions but we did have fun. The place was always packed and it meant that I could try out lots of new material, even if it was somewhat edgy!

I had the Caesars Palace contract to look forward to which was starting in March as I had subsequently been booked for the spring show as well as the summer season…what a result! Maybe he was testing me out and not telling me. The following year was to be yet again another one to remember, but it certainly started off in a very weird way.

I was booked for a week in Yorkshire for an agency called Action Enterprises, performing at a mixture of fun pubs, social clubs and a couple of gay venues thrown in for good measure.

The agency had booked digs for me to stay in for the week with a very nice jolly lady called Avril Barton. She lived in a high rise flat on the outskirts of Leeds and had three cats and a snake. Yes, a frigging snake! The cats never left the flat and the snake she took for a drag every day. Joke!

I am not a pet lover and all these years later I can still remember the smell when I walked in, the hiss and the piss. Using the loo was a blessing! She would get the snake out thinking that I would like it! No, No, No, NO.....

A snake accidentally killed himself.......he bit his tongue!

A gay snake, "Hisssssssss"

Most of the venues were alright. The one I was dreading was the Gemini Club in Huddersfield which was an establishment frequented by men only. It was a bit of a culture shock having never been in a venue like that before, but it turned out to be an absolute scream! I could do camp and gay gags and they loved it.

A gay club... ten men to every man!

Let me get one thing straight! I'm not homophobic, I like living on my own!

I'm not in the closet either guys, I'm claustrophobic!

An agoraphobic man came out. He didn't like it!

I once had a large gay following; but I nipped into a doorway and lost him!

My neighbour is gay, so gay he won't give you a straight answer!

He's behind with the rent and only uses the back door!

He said to me, "I'm having a party, lots of drinks, dancing and hanky panky."I said, "Who's going?" He said, "Just me and you!"

It helped at the end of the act that after the Mick Jagger routine with the tights, I would rip them off as they were held together with Velcro, and went into my In the Navy routine. The Village People, here we come! What I had to do for fifty quid. They loved it.

What a colourful week that was, from a Working Men's Club in Bradford to a cabaret pub in Halifax, The Stone Chair, to a gay club in Huddersfield. Talk about diversity, I haven't worked a gay establishment since, well not knowingly!

117

Chapter Twenty One

Victoria Palace to Caesars Palace

Following my triumphant week with the snake, the cats and the friends of Dorothy, came a comic relief charity night. I returned to the Middlesex Herts and Country Club where I had won the talent show previously. Shane was doing a slot as well as Jeff Stevenson, an excellent stand-up comic who I still see today mainly at sea! I admire Jeff, he has the clever talent to combine, cruising, function work and comedy store work, something I am trying myself as we speak. It is always good performing alongside other comics who are mates as well. We had a fun night and a lot of money was raised for the charity.

A new nightclub had opened in Ipswich called The Dolce Vita and was run by a loveable Italian called Don! I think that was his name and he looked like he had come straight out of the Godfather trilogy! I prayed for a good night as I didn't want to wake up with another horse's head on my pillow!

Then came another special event the biggest one so far. Looking back now it could and should have been the start of something bigger and better for me. That's what a lot of people in the business told me anyway. However, it never really took off for me and I'm still not sure why. I can only assume that it wasn't meant to be.

I auditioned at the Rheingold Club in Soho, London, for the Thames TV variety show, Jim Davidson's Wednesday at 8. Pat Hayley and David Bell were the people I had to impress. The audition went very well once again and I got the chance to appear on one of the shows, I think there were six in the series. They recorded the shows at the Victoria Palace Theatre in London, a great venue. On the bill that night with me were The Nolans, Richard Digance, an American ventriloquist called Ron Lucas, the show company and of course Jim was the host.

Jim opened up with a great routine about the new mobile phone and his mum. Very topical, not the mum bit, but the mobile phone routine! The audience were well pumped up and on I went – very nervous, well wouldn't you be? Especially when, as I stood in the wings just about to go on, Jim happened to mention,

"Remember Mick, seventeen million people are going to be watching this!" Thanks Jim. Nerves are good I know, I held it together, I was so pumped up.

The spot could not have gone better and Jim was kind with his words to the audience as I left the stage. "You're gonna see a lot more of that boy". I could not have wished for a better reaction. What a night!

Afterwards everyone was so complimentary. Before that show my agent, Barry and myself had met with David Morris who was with the Michael Cohen Agency in London. David was to represent me for a while later and I really liked him. Sadly, he is no longer with us. He had a great saying which I never forgot; "Always be unavailable," which I took to mean that the world wants a busy act!

When the show aired on TV in March I was sitting alone in the Merton Hotel in Jersey. Although the actual show went so well on the night we recorded it, you never know what can happen when it comes to the editing, 3:2:1 springs to mind, but the outcome was what I had hoped for. Part of my set was edited out as I had run over time which turned out to be a good thing on reflection.

My set contained the following:

"Here's a beautiful love song recorded by two Spanish firemen, Hose A and Hose B, written by John Miles or as he is known in Spain; Juan Kilometres!"
"Music was my first love….and it will be my last."
GUITAR EXPLODES!!

The reaction on TV was perfect, the sound men did a fab job – unlike 3:2:1. Then into the Quasimodo routine: the band started to play……

"The bells are ringing for me and my girl." Music stops. "It started with a cyst!"

"I thought my troubles were all behind me, then the phone went." The Band miss the cue (as planned). Repeat…… "The phone went!" I picked the phone up and it keeps ringing… "I've got it now!"

"A voice on the phone said, 'Long distance from Notre Dame.' I said, 'It is!"

"I've got some bad news for you." I said, "Don't get my back up!"

"You've been made redundant." I said, "Will I get a lump sum?" "No, but you'll probably get back pay!"

"Me and Esmeralda, we got married and you couldn't see the hump on any of the photos (visual), but we couldn't shut the album!"

"It was last Christmas when it all went wrong, I was at work at the time....."
The Band play; 'Ding Dong Merrily on High'. (I sing the parody)
I fall over and the balloon bursts (hump).

It came over so well on the television, the feeling after watching it was of relief, excitement and great satisfaction. It's not easy watching yourself on the box!

The Caesars Palace Spring Show was about to start. During rehearsals I flew back to London to meet with David Morris and Michael Cohen in their London office to negotiate a contract. They were more than happy to take me on and they were due to fly out to Jersey to see me in the show and then the contracts would subsequently be signed.

My expectations were short-lived. It never happened and to this day I don't know why? This business can have you flying one minute and letting you down the next. Maybe somebody else was involved.... who knows?

It was a huge disappointment for me at the time. It would have given me such a lift. Every now and again my confidence would get knocked for whatever reason....but anyway we moved on and I had the summer at Caesars Palace in Jersey to look forward to.

I was working in the production show as well as performing a twenty minute spot in each half. On most nights something different would happen, helping to add and re-vamp new lines, keeping the act fresh throughout. It was to be a turning point in my career and I moved up a level working in a more prestigious venue, which was full to capacity every night.

Being at Caesars Palace was a big boost for me. I felt that I was moving in the right direction and that my act was steadily improving due to working in such a professional environment.

I was missing my family of course and couldn't wait for the school holidays when they could all come over and we could be together. I was away seven and a half months in all which was too long and I was looking forward to being back home again.

There were numerous shows on the island starring many talented artistes. The Monday lunches for the Variety Club, the Saturday open mike comedy sessions and the midnight shows that were on now and again, so there was a lot going on.

The Palace was open six nights a week and every other Sunday I would work in a hotel in St. Helier. It was a very busy time for me performance wise and Jersey was a great place to be. The cast were superb in my debut year at the Palace and included: Stuart Gillies, Diane Cousins, Billy Kelly, six dancers and the superb and wonderful Roger Bara Orchestra.

Stuart helped me no end in keeping my feet firmly on the ground and he made sure that my standards didn't drop. He and his lovely family have remained great friends of mine to this day. He is a true pro through and through and I'm sure many of you will remember him from his success on TV's Opportunity Knocks Song Writers Show. Diane, a singer and comedienne extraordinaire, was a very strong act and Billy Kelly was one of the funniest guys I have ever worked with. Such a naturally funny man, he did like a drink though and sadly he is no longer with us today.

The format started with a production routine to open each half then us four artistes performed an opening song together with one or two funnies thrown in. The acts would do two spots, one in each half. Stuart closed the first half and yours truly the second, just before the finale. It was certainly a big ending to a show that lasted for over three hours.

We wore top hats and tails, all in white, me with a top hat that was just a touch too big, a white cane and I was told to keep it serious and not mess about! Yeah right! The more I tried to play it straight the more the audience laughed. The stairs would come down onto the stage from above by hydraulics – it was quite spectacular.

My first spot would consist of an assortment of gags about all and sundry. I gradually built up a repertoire about Jersey itself, the place, the locals, the Police and so forth.

Front page news in the local Jersey Evening Post - Cow hit by lorry and they didn't name the Cow!

50,000 tonnes of straw were pinched from a farm today in Jersey and the Police believe that a vehicle was involved!

I'd close the first half with Diana and Quasimodo, they always went down well. The exploding guitar would open the second half, but midway through the season I had to drop it from the act. It was too dangerous apparently, someone would eventually have a heart attack...... allegedly!

I did a vasectomy gag with a newspaper which was very visual and funny, you had to be there! Also, the Indian routine with the Custer's glass eye gag.

My good friend Lee Carroll wrote a lovely French girlfriend routine for me which went down really well with the French connection in Jersey. I would later use this on the Michael Barrymore show for the BBC. With my Tom Jones, Freddie Star, Norman Wisdom and Mick Jagger routines adding new stand-up and a rock 'n'roll medley to close, my act was continuing to improve and getting tighter all the time.

On the very last night of the season the show was somewhat different. Quite a few of the audience had seen the show before so we changed a few things to spice it up a bit. I would do the Diana parody with Diane Cousins and it was certainly different! It threw me somewhat especially when she forgot her lines!

Quasimodo was a bit off the wall; the orchestra came out with cloaks on and did the parody with me. They had secretly put the music on tape and it brought the house down!

To the Band Leader, "Can you give me an F..., a U..., a C..., F U C me walking down the street....."

I'd now like to sing "The Party's Over' in 'F' or is it The F'ing Party's Over!"

Here's a song by the pregnant ballerina, 'I Should Have Danced All Night!'

I only have eyes for you but you should see what I've got for your sister!

Here's a beautiful song... how can I tell you that I love you when you're sitting on my face!

Lester Piggott wouldn't go into his cell. They had to blindfold him, turn him round three times and then back him in!

Lots more ad libs and throw away gags followed, plus some banter from the punters. Then Stuart did a song which featured a Pas De Deux where I took the female part, dressed in a tutu alongside Amir, the male dancer! This was done very seriously and we rehearsed for some weeks and the audience loved it! It was hysterical – you had to be there!

With the excellent dancers and production, the show was always a hit and I could not have wished for a better start in my debut season at Caesars Palace. It became a run of five years and I enjoyed working there tremendously. The icing on the cake at the end of that season was winning the Best Comedian Award at the Variety Club Awards Dinner. My dear mum was so proud and I felt that I had improved as an act and gained valuable experience that summer.

Towards the end of the season, Barry, my agent, had arranged for David Llewellyn, the P&O cruise booker, to come over and see me. On the strength of my twenty minute second half performance David was suitably impressed and he booked me for a cruise on the *Canberra* for the first leg of a world cruise in January, from Southampton to New Orleans.

When the season, which included spring, summer and autumn was over, it was so good to get back to my family. I came back down to Earth with a bump as far as work was concerned. I did a run of twenty-one shows in twenty-three days for a South West agent called John Mills. I say South West, one of the venues was in Slough! I think the loveable John was a part-time travel agent as well!

Butlins came calling and I took the long drive from Ipswich to Minehead, taking almost a day to get there, the M25 was now open...sometimes!

Barnum's was a great vibrant cabaret room and the crowd could be somewhat loud and hostile so I had to go in strong once again, the visual and vocal side of my act paid off! The gig was a long way to go but well worth it as the night had gone so well.

Pauline threw a surprise party for me when I returned home from Jersey. It was a wonderful night and she had done me proud. Shane and lots of other artistes had turned up. I had never been away for so long before and never have again since. It was so good to be home.

Chapter Twenty-Two

Waves of Laughter

Just as I thought that things could not get any better and top that year, along came a world cruise, or rather the first leg of it, then a second season at the Palace and another big TV special. I was really nervous but excited at the challenge of embarking on the *Canberra* and not knowing what the format was.

It was certainly an eye-opener when I was told how much material was needed. Six different shows, a fifteen minute welcome aboard show, a fifteen minute farewell variety show and four half hour shows in between. Two and a half hours of material. I was doing once again more spots than the proverbial welder!

You can imagine the terror I felt inside! I had probably only performed around forty-five to sixty minutes up until then. I had to adapt quickly and expand my existing material and also get help from others. I even had to sing a bit, not easy when you can't! I was like Van Gogh – no ear for music!

It was a new beginning performing for P&O on the prestigious *Canberra* but it was fortunate that I could obtain material from around the ship itself. This has become a pattern for all the cruises that I have done over the years. Others helped me with stock lines as well during that first cruise.

I remember closing the last show with Roger Whittaker's The Last Farewell, sad I know, but I wanted to do my time. I've never sung it since!!

We were living in G Deck on *Canberra*. We had to share communal showers and toilets which is hard to believe in today's world but nevertheless it was a great experience and one I will never forget.

I've got a nice cabin, I'm on Millionaires Row... Deck One!

I'm on the odd side, numbers that is!

I'm in the Jacques Cousteau Suite!

I get the Bends when I go to bed at night!

My cabin is right at the front of the ship, in fact it comes to a point!

I thought my television was a porthole!

Looking back, it was quite a feather in my cap to get a leg of a world cruise on my first introduction to the high seas. I do thrive on a challenge and that was certainly a big one.

In today's cruising world more often than not acts need two forty-five minute slots, two very strong ones hopefully, and after all these years I have added much more stand-up to my act and the props have gone.

A lot of the acts I know have turned to cruising due to the decline in the bread and butter gigs on the mainland. Many fall into the trap of thinking that cruising is easier work, but I have learnt from experience that a cruising audience seems to expect that little bit more. They have paid a lot of money for their cruising holiday and expect a higher standard and quite rightly so.

An act once asked me, "How do I get on P&O?" I replied, "Go to any Travel Agent!"

I always looked forward to the local clubs and didn't feel any extra pressure performing in front of a home crowd.

A gig at Norwich City Football Club for a sponsor's dinner for Anglia TV was a highlight, but a gig at an RAF Camp in Bedfordshire stood out, the reason being that no black gags were to be told as the Sergeant Major was black. Surely this is discrimination of the highest order. I don't do black gags anyway, but I guess the gag about the black man who was being blackmailed and was the black sheep of the family from Blackpool, being taken away to Blackheath Police Station in a black maria was blackballed!

The cabaret clubs, La Taverna at Epping, the Silver Skillet at Maidenhead, Victorias near Maidstone and the Downtown Restaurant in Rotherhythe were all becoming firm favourites and I enjoyed performing there on a regular basis.

Because of the success of my previous year at Caesars Palace, Dick Ray asked me back for the sequel! It was yet again another wonderful season, Billy Kelly returned together with a singer from the North East called Stephen Lee Garden. He had just won the New Faces Grand Final, so this was indeed a coup for the guv'nor. I would say on stage that he had now become a household name, but I knew him when he was Stephen Lee Window Box! He didn't find it funny, but he was a great singer none the less. The format was much the same as it had been a winning one for years and so successful.

The dancers, five girls and one boy would open, then us acts would then do a bit together, our rendition of Make Em Laugh and then Billy would do his stuff. He never did any one liners but would tell funny stories instead. He would flower these stories somewhat and he could make a one line gag last for minutes. He was a great story teller.

Diane Cousins sang and did comedy as well. She was and still is a very strong act to follow but I knew the audience would be well warmed up. She would do the business every time. I would then do my slot, an opening number, then sing New York into Neighbours, which was very topical at the time. Lots of stand up on various subjects gradually adding even more to the Jersey routine. The roads are very small and narrow in Jersey with a maximum speed limit of 40 mph but in some places this was reduced to 20 mph!

They say the Germans were here during the War. Where did they park?!

I was driving around Jersey today, reaching speeds of up to 15 mph!

They don't bury the dead in Jersey, they give them a driving licence!

When you come to a small roundabout the sign says: 'Filter In Turn'. I waited half an hour for a car today!

I turned right and took someone's washing off the line!

We opened the second half of the show with all the cast performing the Tommy Steele classic, Flash Bang Wallop! Great fun.

Billy would do his second stand up followed by the dancers performing part of *Bolero*'s Carmen.

126

I was to follow this wonderful piece so I had this brilliant idea of coming on to the music from Carmen, dragging an inflatable doll behind me, dressed of course, and throwing her around the stage. I then did a Michael Jackson skit, wearing a latex mask made especially for me when I was back home, doing a parody of Bad, changing it to Mad. Stephen closed his second spot with a Phantom medley, then all the cast finished the extravaganza with the usual big production number. Marvellous!

The Monday Clubs and charity nights were once again in full flow and I was fortunate enough to get the Best Comedian Award again for the second year in succession. I was getting some of my material written by the aforementioned funny guy Lee Carroll, writing some stuff myself and adding to it all the time. Funny moments on stage would just happen and then become part of the act.

Michael Barrymore's Saturday Night Out for the BBC was being recorded at the Fort Regent in Jersey and I was booked to do it. Lee wrote the routine for me and I put it in the show at Caesars to get it honed in for the TV show. Although it went ok, it wasn't as good as Wednesday at 8. The Victoria Palace Theatre in London had a great atmosphere but the Fort Regent in Jersey didn't, it was more like an indoor arena. Nevertheless, again, it was very good experience for me, the routine was clean, clever and very apt for Jersey.

Lee gave me a great opening line to the audience:

Do you want some good news? And they would shout out Yes!

Then I would grab a box of Good News Chocolates (Do you remember them?) and throw some to the audience! It would be no good now as they stopped making them years ago, they probably have a different name now, shame. Good gag! I then did the French girlfriend routine that Lee wrote for me, donning a beret and a string of onions around my neck!

I took her to a French Restaurant... 'Le Petit Chef!'

She had frog's legs and chicken breasts... but a lovely personality!

She said, "Will you run me home?" I beat her by twenty minutes!

127

She waffled in broken English, "I have something that you want, you have something that I want. What you want is what I have. What I have is what you want." I said, "What do you want?" She said, "I want your baby." I said, "I haven't got one!"

She started to cry so I said, "Are you crying because you're in love with me?" She said, "No, no...... it's these bloody onions!"

It was a very good routine and very appropriate for Jersey.

Michael Barrymore, his wonderful PA Jenny Leah, and some of the crew from his TV show came to see the show at Caesars Palace one night together with John Bergerac Nettles, Sean Arnold and the gang from the hit BBC programme. The Caesars show had a very good reputation on Jersey and there was hardly ever an empty seat in the house. VIP's made it that little bit special. I have this memory of Michael, who was a great entertainer at the time, drunk as a skunk at the Grand Hotel in St. Helier trying to light a cigarette with little success. Oh how the mighty have fallen.......

Once again it was so nice to get back home to my family at the end of the season, the homeboy was ready for home. Work wise it would be a bit of an anticlimax being back on the road again. I had been spoilt with no travelling for all those months.

Unfortunately the flip side to success is that being away from home was starting to take its toll and the strain was beginning to show in my relationship with Pauline.

Chapter Twenty-Three

Apologies For Being Funny

I went back for a third season on the bounce at Caesars, the trilogy! I know it's getting boring now, but quite the opposite for me! My act had grown and improved no end, being resident there for the last two summers had made me raise my game and I could feel myself steadily getting better all the time. The discipline that was needed to keep to time, all the production numbers and sketches and regularly updating and adding material was so rewarding.

It was another fun filled season. It was a World Cup year and Stuart Gillies had returned and he represented Scotland, because he's Scottish! The Irish funny man Pat Mooney was representing Ireland of course, then there was me cheering on the England team, praying that we didn't go to penalties!

Once again it was the usual format, the dancers opened, then the three of us with a song and a few funnies. Pat Mooney was sure to get a laugh with his own Irish brand of humour. A production routine followed, combining rock 'n' roll, Grease, Elvis and a motorbike on stage to boot which was loud to say the least! I would do my stuff and I changed the content somewhat for obvious reasons as there were lots of return holiday makers. The Quasimodo sketch had improved by adding the five dancers who were now all in robes. Seeing six Quasimodo's dancing around the floor to George Michael's, Wake Me Up Before You Go Go must have looked funny. It certainly felt funny and I would try and knock into them, they didn't like that though, its comedy luvvie! Stuart would close the first half in his own inimitable style, he was everybody's cup of tea, a true professional through and through.

We did a World Cup routine, the three of us, gags flying everywhere:

The Scots will be back home before their postcards!

The English Manager has picked his team for the World Cup... Brazil!

The Irish made a sub. They held up the number 11 and they all came off!

There were many more and we wore our respective football kits. Not a pretty sight but we had a ball....get it?!

Another production routine involved the girls doing a Superwoman routine and then Stuart and I coming on as Batman and Robin! It was very funny and great fun to do. Del boy and Rodney, eat your heart out!

Once again, the finale was a big production number with top hat and tails, the sticks and stairs, then time for bed.

That summer despite those missed penalties and the tears of Gazza, was still a big win for us as far as the season was concerned and we had lots of fun. The dancers were in my rock 'n' roll routine which was now choreographed superbly by Stuart's beautiful wife, Rachel. The routine was fast, furious and funny and I would get pushed, slapped and kicked, but all for a good cause....comedy!

The eighties could not have been busier, constant one-nighters and summer seasons with TV thrown in for good measure every now and then. Unfortunately, all this work and travelling, trying to build my career and make a name for myself, finally took its toll in my personal life.

My marriage to Pauline had broken down. Being away from home that much was not ideal and did not help our relationship. Success comes at a price and sometimes it is not a nice one. It is fair to say that I did feel guilty in those early years, travelling far and wide to earn a good living and achieve the success and recognition that I hoped for. There wasn't much time for a regular social life and I probably became a victim of my own success if the truth be known.

It was a very difficult time and for a long while my personal life became a mess. The thought of those dark days whilst trying to make people laugh still haunt me. It certainly makes me appreciate what I have today.

Leaving the family home but still trying to keep a strong relationship with my children was difficult. We all have to make sacrifices sometimes. Today, thank goodness, life is nowhere near as hectic.

I have never been a moody or depressive sort of guy. I am always trying to be positive when things aren't quite going my way. The next five years weren't easy or particularly happy ones. I rented a room in a house in Ipswich, then a flat in

Felixstowe, went back to living with my mum and dad for a while, this was all in between working away some of the time.

Nobody wants to feel down or depressed but it can creep up on you without knowing and you have to be strong, pick yourself up, dust yourself down and keep going. Don't let the bastards get you down! Family and good friends are everything to me.

I am in a great place today but those dark days on my own, desperate to see my children and having to do so well on stage was somewhat difficult. I was sometimes asking myself, what is it all about? What am I actually doing this for? What is the meaning of life? It was a long time ago and the relationship I have with my children today could not be stronger. They are my rock and I hope I am theirs!

I had nearly twenty good years with my first love Pauline and I don't have any bad memories. It was a great shame the marriage didn't work out but one very important thing is we produced two fantastic children whom we love so dearly along with our two beautiful grandchildren.

Time is a healer they say.....no more apologies for being funny.

Chapter Twenty-Four

Now is the Summer of my Discontent

After that third season at Caesars I went into Soho. Ooh I say Matron. No, not to a house of horizontal refreshment where they sell broth, but to a Sky studio. It was the early days of Sky TV and a programme called Jameson Tonight was being recorded in this very small studio seating around forty people, literally taken off the street!

It was a very informal chat cum variety show with Derek Jameson and his sidekick, my old buddy Shane. I remember the show well, it felt like working in a Comedy Store atmosphere, as we know it today.

I had a leather suitcase very old in appearance and knowing that there would be a lack of atmosphere in the studio, I decided that when the first laugh didn't come from the audience I would open the suitcase and recorded laughter would come over the PA system. I would then shut the case and the laughter would stop. Nothing new but very effective! After those few planted laughs I got the routine slightly out and messed up the timing so there was an even bigger laugh from the punters. You had to be there!

My entrance was me walking down the staircase, holding the suitcase and I was on the phone, one of those early brick type mobiles.

These new mobile phones are brilliant ladies and gentlemen; then bringing their attention to the case....but the batteries are a pain!

What a nightmare trying to park in Soho – I saw a bloke lying in the gutter and asked him, "What are you doing?" He said, "I've found a space and sent the wife home for the car!"

I opened the case for a false laugh!

A homeless person is in the street with a sign saying 'Falklands War Hero'. I throw some coins into his cap and he says, "Gracias Signor!"

I open the case for another false laugh!

132

I have a yuppy girlfriend and she wanted to 'work out', so I said, "Get a Jane Fonda video." So she went and got 'On Golden Pond!' (This was 1990!)

She started jogging ten miles a day and by Sunday she'll be in Chelmsford!

I did a few visual impressions and all went very well;

Phone to my ear: "You really hurt me." I put the phone down. 'That was my dentist!'

Vincent Van Gogh on his holidays; cock the sunglasses so they are only on one ear!

There were many silly off the wall visual lines. This was part of me in those days especially having Zany as a stage name! The recording was over in a flash but I enjoyed the almost off the cuff approach.

Another obscure TV programme came up called Bushell on the Box. This was another very informal and pleasant experience with the then Sun newspaper entertainment columnist, Gary Bushell. He was a lovely guy and we had such a laugh recording the show in his house in South London. He often gave me a plug in dispatches in the paper and I thank him for that.

The recording went really well, it was just a cameo really so I felt no real pressure, it was fun.

My Granddad is in hospital waiting for a by-pass and we are worried about the protestors!

I parked at the pay and display car park, the M25! I was on there so long I got clamped!

My girlfriend's got that Mad Cow disease!

I've been eating beef all my life, it's not affected moo.....me!

I'm getting my hair cut for a film. I'm off to the cinema tomorrow!

I've been to see a shrink, he's very good. I used to be 6 ft. 8'!

And to end: Here's a little thought...... here's another one!

It had been another year to look back on with great satisfaction work wise, adding to my act and gaining more and more experience.

Every so often a gig can come along and I wished I hadn't taken it. I was asked to do the Variety Club of Great Britain Golf Society Stag Dinner. Pat Mooney put me forward for it and he seemed to think that the material from the summer show in Jersey would be just right for that night. I learnt the hard way.

From 10pm to 11pm three established comedians did their slots and all went fine for them. Fun and games around the tables followed, then the Auction took forever! My time came at 12.30am, it was way too late. It's a different story now, but way back then......they say that you learn from the bad gigs and hopefully you do. I got away with it, but only just. Fail to prepare......

I hope I see you all again... but not as a group!

I wouldn't give this spot to a Leopard!

To see the year out there were more Christmas functions and office parties, a new venue, The Kingfisher Country Club at Kingswinford near Wolverhampton. A good venue and the accommodation was thrown in as well which made it a very enjoyable run.

It was back to the high seas on the *Canberra* and we visited Yalta and Odessa. Russia was now in change and the streets were very quiet with people selling all sorts of things. I remember bringing back some memorabilia for my son James, a Russian officer's hat, helmet and a gun! (How did I get that through Customs?) No more six different slots this time just a welcome aboard show, a farewell show and a couple of full shows in between, still two hours in total mind you!

A granddad was telling his grandson that he had some army memorabilia up in the loft. A helmet, a rifle and he even had an army trench coat wrapped around the tank. The little boy exclaimed, "you've got a tank up in the loft as well granddad?!"

The one nighters were still thriving and the holiday park circuit was also busy, smaller private sites on the Essex and Yarmouth coastlines were added to the more established Haven, Pontins and Butlins Centres.

Spring and summer came around and proved to be eventful to say the least. I returned yet again to Caesars Palace but only for a few weeks this time. Thinking about it I should have applied for residency back in 1980, I could have been a Jersey Boy by now! (Isn't that a musical?)

It was only a short spring show and I teamed up once again with the very funny Billy Kelly and a wonderful singer and good friend called Scott Paige who is the brother of Paul Wagner, or Billy Connolly tribute as I like to think of him.

In June of that year I went to Blackpool to star in the Mystique show at the Pleasure Beach. I say star very lightly – this was not to be my finest or happiest hour for a number of reasons. I have come across a few people that are in the business who have made, shall we say, life a little difficult for me.

It was a tough start especially the opening night, going on stage at around 11.45pm after the Mystique show had finished! Can you imagine the mayhem and noise when the show company came out and some people were leaving to go home, thinking the night was over? It was way too late to go on stage at that time.

John Butcher and Gloria Gee had come to Jersey to see me at Caesars the year before. They loved it and I thought that I would be working in a similar role in Blackpool. Unfortunately, it was as bad as Jersey was good. Mystique was a fabulous extravaganza fronted by Russ Stevens and it contained illusion and dance and was an amazing show.

At 11.45 pm at Caesars Palace the entertainment would be coming to an end with a big production number to close. Not at Blackpool, oh no, let's put the comic on at the end and watch him struggle somewhat then die on his arse!

I had a meeting after that opening night, the next day in fact, and the timings were changed. It was agreed that I would now do a first spot at the end of the first half and then a second spot at the end. That way at least the audience had some idea of what to expect after the Mystique show had finished. Fortunately it was a lot better, I closed the first half with my Diana and Quasimodo routines which always did the business.

It was always going to be hard after three fantastic years in Jersey. It would be difficult to top that and so it proved. It was better performing the two spots but I never enjoyed it. The format of Mystique had changed that year, compared to previous years much to my misfortune, but it was a learning curve for sure.

Outside of the Pleasure Beach I had a much more enjoyable time, making friends with many of the artistes who were working at the time in Blackpool. There were quite a few star performers around and the Blackpool Golf Society was formed that summer with comedians who included; Mick Miller, Mike Doyle, George King, Franklyn James, Keith Harris and many more fabulous acts.

Although Pauline and I had separated she still came up with Claire and James for a few weeks and I was so glad to see them.

When things are going well you feel on top of the world but when they are not it can be heartbreaking especially when you are not with your family.

Sometimes when you are feeling down and life isn't going according to plan you need special people around you, people who understand the business. I'm sure that we have all been there at some stage. Sometimes a good kick up the arse and positive thinking works wonders!

I thought that I would just get through this season and things would improve, and they did. The next Summer I was back at the Palace in Jersey. There is a God!

Chapter Twenty-Five

Déjà Vu

The disappointment of my Blackpool experience was a bit hard to take but the success and satisfaction of being one of the stars of Caesars Palace in Jersey for three consecutive years made sure that I stayed focused and confident.

Confidence is everything in this business. You need all the bravado that you can manage and as I have said before don't let the bastards get you down and never let them smell the fear!

After Blackpool there was a ferry crossing from Southampton to Cherbourg on the *Stenna Normandy*, not quite *Canberra* but only one spot!

A particularly interesting gig at Fakenham Community Centre was next. I know what you're thinking, name dropper! It was unusual in the fact that many of the audience were Americans, probably from the nearby bases. It was a chance to adapt my act and probably unknowingly, it prepared me for American audiences on cruise ships today.

I like Fakenham...... My girlfriend, she likes faking'em!

Another busy year loomed with gigs at the regular clubs, holiday parks and restaurants and a particularly enjoyable show at the HMS Naval Base in Portsmouth.

Our football Manager took the team to Portsmouth to show them what a 'Victory' looks like!

I couldn't wait for the new season to start at the Palace as my memories of that last summer in Blackpool were nicely fading into obscurity.

Now I would be working back in a team and not just on my own. There were other performers and dancers and a brilliant orchestra but more importantly a happy and successful environment. There was not an egotistical tosser in sight!

The line-up for the 1992 season at the Palace was myself, Terry Denton and Mia Carla. Terry had played the Palace before and was a great act, one of the boys. He had to go on at the end, not always easy after nearly three hours of entertainment. He never complained however and just got on with it and did the business. I had met Mia Carla when I was in Blackpool the previous summer. She was working at the Viking Hotel, aka The Talk of the Coast, two nights a week. She had shown an interest in working in Jersey so I told the boss and she was in. Mia is certainly not a laid back act and is very in your face, but funny. She was a larger than life character, in more ways than one and she did a great fitness work-out routine in the show with the dancers which was hysterical.

There was a production number to open followed by the three of us doing our rendition of I'm so excited! Terry opened and closed, Mia did her bit including the fitness routine class! She said she wanted to work out every day! She wanted to work out why she's not fit!

They say you are what you eat. She must have eaten the Vicar of Dibley!

She's on two diets now. There was not enough food on the first!

Her favourite musical instrument at school was the Dinner Bell!

I told her to try horse riding, that's good for losing weight. She did and the horse lost four stone!

I did my normal two spots but added some different material as I had been there two years previously. I had to, I needed to keep it fresh. I added some more visual and vocal content which included; Nat King Cole, Stevie Wonder, Frank Sinatra and Tom Jones, not serious singing I hasten to add!

Terry and I did a Blues Brothers routine to open the second half of the show with the production team, followed by a ballet routine with Mia and myself. She was the big fairy because she was big and I wore a pink tutu because I was the ballerina! Mia did a rendition on her own of Nobody Loves a Fairy When She's Old! Then we did our beautiful, very funny Pas de deux followed by the extra-large balloon sketch where we rolled the balloon around each other and I ended up through her legs, then the balloon burst. I then tried to lift her, no joy there, so she picked me up and carried me off! Hilarious…you had to be there!

To finish, there was a big finale production number and we all ended up on the stairs, except the fairy!

It was to be my last season in Jersey. Times were changing and the audience numbers were falling. Over the last couple of years artists from the Palace were being loaned out to some of the hotels and holiday centres, so more people could see the acts in the comfort of their own hotel and not venture out and pay money to see the full show at the Palace. It was still a great time and Jersey will always hold many happy memories for me. The people I met and the friends I still have, but above all the job satisfaction was second to none.

Sadly, Terry Denton and Billy Kelly were both diagnosed with cancer and passed away in 1993. They were both true professionals, good friends, very funny and great people to be around.

I still miss them today.

Chapter Twenty-Six

I'm in Panto.....Oh No You're Not!

From Jersey to P&O's *Sea Princess*, a wonderful medium sized ship. I took the rock'n'roll routine with the dancers on there and it was a big hit. Unfortunately though due to my naivety I made a gross error of judgement.

We did a crew show in the International Lounge at midnight, all went well and I closed with the rock'n'roll number. I went into my Mick Jagger routine where I used a large sponge for Jagger's lips. Then I would put the sponge down the front of my black tights to enhance my package like Rudolf Nureyev, so to speak, which was always a guaranteed laugh! A touch of the Benny Hills as everyone loved Benny Hill at the time, and not forgetting that this was a midnight show after all!

The crew loved it and I received a very nice letter from the Staff Captain thanking me for my contribution to a great night.

When it came to my show to the paying passengers I kept it in and complaints were made. To be fair I had been in two minds whether to do it or not, especially the sponge down the tights bit, but all and sundry, including the Cruise Director urged me on to do it as it had gone so well at the Crew Show. Anyway, after the complaints, he never backed me up and took no responsibility at all. I won't name and shame him but I never forgave the weedy tosser!

Looking back now I should have followed my gut feeling and gone with my instinct not to do it. I learnt a hard lesson from that episode.....if in doubt, leave it out!

Nevertheless, I had to travel down to Southampton and meet with the booker, David. It was four years before I cruised with the Company again.

December of that year saw me work for the last time at Victoria's in Kent. I had ten wonderful years there and it had always been a great gig. Sadly, I had a minor disagreement with the management. I had asked to pull out of a Christmas Day show for family reasons as I wanted to be with my kids. I lost the gig and was never to return. It's a fickle business sometimes!

However, the year finished with my first pantomime, a Nick Thomas and Jon Conway production. They had seen me the previous summer at the Palace in

Jersey and were suitably impressed to give me the pantomime and a summer season the following year.

It was Snow White and the Seven Dwarfs in Cambridge with Geoff Capes and the two stars from Home and Away, Bruce Roberts and Dee Smart. I played Muddles and it was fun, twelve shows a week! Oh yes it was!

The summer of 1993 included a Haven floorshow, a variety show working five nights a week in Torquay, five nights a week in Weymouth and a third week in Scarborough, Sundays to Thursdays. The South coast venues were family orientated and the Scarborough venues were mainly adult only.

It was not quite the class of Jersey and the travelling was horrendous. I was living here, there and everywhere, no fixed abode was my permanent address! That was over twenty years ago now and was to be my last summer season.

With no cruising for a few years it was the bread and butter gigs that I had to concentrate on. Pontins were still in full swing at the time and their venues included; Pakefield at Lowestoft, Seacroft at Hemsby, Osmington Bay in Weymouth, Sand Bay in Weston-Super-Mare, Barton Hall and Wall Park in Torquay, Blackpool and Wick Ferry, Bournemouth.

Warners were also to become regular venues for me over the next ten years or so and unlike Pontins, they were all adult only! The venues included; Gunton Hall and Corton in Lowestoft, Bodelwyddan Castle in North Wales, Cricket St. Thomas in Somerset, Lakeside and Sinah Warren at Hayling Island, Nidd Hall in Harrogate, Bembridge and Norton Grange on the Isle of White.

There were also cameo performances at the Newmarket Cabaret Club, Lakeside Country Club and Caesars Palace at Luton with the Southlanders. Do you remember their hit, I am a Mole and I Live in a Hole? No, nor do I!

With football and golf clubs also a feature all was going very nicely thank you, with work that is!

There was no lady in my life and seeing the children was not always easy. The travelling around did not help and I had no regular home for them to come and stay. It was somewhat harrowing and I hated the fact that I could not see them on a more regular basis. Making a career in show business did certainly have its drawbacks.

I sometimes wonder what effect it had on me and the children, as I said before, I am a home-boy but it wasn't possible to make a living as a full-time comedian working only in the East Anglian area.

Twenty years on and so much has changed, there are no more summer seasons or pantomimes for me now. Cruising is mainly limited to a few days at a time and not weeks and any gigs I do are mostly there and back in the same night. There are no more pro digs or staying in hotels. Most of the cabaret venues and clubs are not there anymore and the number of holiday parks has dwindled somewhat.

Cruising is a flourishing market and still is my main income. Nowadays, to be on a ship for just a few days at a time suits me fine. Also, if someone is travelling with me it makes a world of difference as I have always found it difficult to be on my own killing time.

1994 came along, no cruising, no summer seasons but the gigs were in full flow. Butlins provided adult weekends at Bognor with Bernard Manning, Roger de Courcey, Mike Reid and many others. I would perform in the afternoon after the punters had their lunchtime drink which meant we could let rip and get stuck in! The visual impressions would be, shall we say, a little more risqué!

My experience of working Stag and Hen nights really helped especially with the ad libs and put downers! Adult weekends could be scary but oh so satisfying as well. It felt so good to win a pumped up audience over, especially when they're having a go at you. The drive home was better and much more rewarding!

Am I lucky or is he always here?

I was gonna do an impression of an idiot, but he's beaten me to it!

Nine million sperm and his had to win!

When you were circumcised they threw the wrong bit away!

He'll never get piles; he's the perfect arsehole!

A week in the Birmingham area followed with various clubs and the odd night club in the mix, the only downside being the pro digs. It was a week's money though and I needed it, as you do.

The Watney Roadshows now became Courage Roadshows, they were still fun to do, working with other acts, and a backing band to boot. Once again I was constantly adding new material and not resting on my laurels. I wanted to update all the time keeping my act fresh.

I soon got to the point where I could do a total stand-up set or use the band for the visual and vocal side of the act. Sometimes I had to use backing tapes but using live music with a talented band is obviously much better. The comedy can be more unpredictable and off the cuff....keep music live.

I never like the act to look like it has been set up too much. I believe it should appear as if I am making it up or improvising strange as that may sound. Ad libbing with the audience is also a big hit most of the time!

With Pontins and Butlins being regular haunts, it was a pleasant diversion to do some theatre dates. One such tour was with the very talented Joe Longthorne. He is a great vocal impressionist and he starred in his own show back in Jersey during my debut year of 1980. I have always been an ardent fan of his and was so chuffed to support him in such theatres as; Sheffield City Hall, The Swansea Grand and Nottingham Theatre Royal to name but a few. He would invite me to his dressing room to meet his family after some of the gigs, the Romany's.

Do gypsy's pay by traveller's cheques?

It was at this time that I used to do the sponsors cabaret for Ipswich Town Football Club, one spot before the match and one afterwards. Winning meant an easier second spot, but losing was not quite the same. Whilst working at Portman Road I managed to get my son James to be mascot twice! The first was at a Tottenham game and the other was a home match against West Bromwich Albion.

Testimonials were fun to do and they would include a golf day as well, what could be better! I remember doing several shows when the great Bobby Robson was present. He was a great man, a legend, and my hero.

Jim Davidson's Sinderella came to Ipswich, it was a very funny blue version of Cinderella, and I went to see it several times, it was hilarious! Jim came to Ipswich many times with his stand-up shows, mind you Ipswich is the Mecca of entertainment! I worked with Jim on several occasions in those days and it was always nice to catch up with him.

Although there was no summer season to speak of I started to go back to Jersey for two nights each week to do both Pontins venues, Portelet and Plemont Bay, and two Modern Hotels, The Mayfair and The Metropole. Four shows in two nights – luvley! Either side of these it would be the usual suspects, Pontins, Haven and Butlins with their latest acquisition being Bayswater in London!

It did seem strange driving to the middle of London to do a Butlins gig but it was a fun night. It wasn't fun trying to park though!

I solved my parking problem. I bought a parked car!

You don't get a ticket parking in London, you get a medal!

I parked the car on double yellow lines and asked the Traffic Warden, "Can I park here?" He said, "No." I said, "But all these other cars are parked here?" And he said, "They didn't ask!"

A Traffic Warden was laid out in the Morgue. The Coroner said, "Dead" and the Traffic Warden said, "I'm not dead." And the Coroner replied, "Sorry Sir, I've started the paperwork!"

Gigs at Brighton Trades and Labour Club, Handsworth Horticultural Club, Haven at Seasalter in North Kent, Junior Ranks at Colchester Garrison, all kept my feet firmly on the ground. Any sign of stardom seemed light years away, maybe my chance had gone? Had my moment come along before I was ready? I was beginning to think so.

The Chateau Plasir Show
Jersey 1986

Backstage at the
Chateau with 'Reg'

'Get me the number plate...'

Me and Shane at the
Chateau Plaisir, 1986

Rocky & Rambo

1986 at the Chateau Plaisir

1986 Midnight Show,
Quasimodo routine

1986 Midnight Show, Jersey,
'The exploding guitar'

Mick Miller's 'Noddy' routine at his
birthday party, Ritz Hotel, 1986

147

Mick Miller's Birthday Party
- Love the syrup, Mick!

The second half of the
season at the Chateau
with the 'Young Brothers'

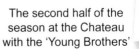

All the gang at
Mount Pleasant
Airport

Having fun
after the show
with the
squaddies

Simon & Shane
in the Chinook

Winter in the Falklands
1987

1987 January,
Port Stanley Falklands

Mount Kent,
Falkland Isles

Me on Mount Alice,
Falklands

Me with Karen & Paula,
Sweet Illusion, 1987

Me with Jay, Cetan Mani
1987

1987 The Modern Hotel
Travelling Show, Jersey

Me with the guv'nor Paul,
his wife Kay and Rachel Gillies,
Jersey 1987

Me batting at a charity
cricket match in St. Johns,
Jersey, 2nd August 1987

1987, The Modern Hotel Travelling Show

Outside Charity event for Cancer Research, Jersey 1987.
That's what I call a Sun Hat!

An impromptu moment with Claire
at the Monday Variety Club luncheon, 1987

153

Performing 'Diana'
with Diane at
Caesars Palace in 1988

Performing the pas de deux
with Amir at Caesars Palace,
Jersey 1988

Myself, Stuart, Diane, Billy
and James, backstage at
Caesars, 1988

Sugar Babes, Caesars
1988

154

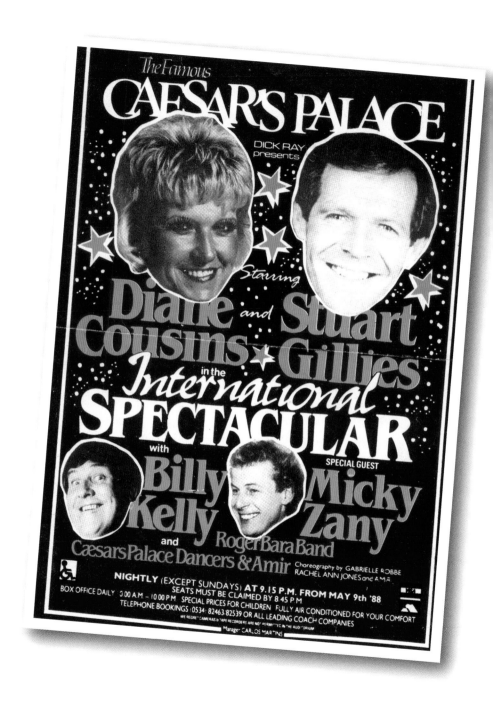

1989
Show Company
at the Palace

The Show Company, Cae-
sars Palace 1989 at the
Variety Club Dinner

Me & Billy at the bar
at Caesars

Me with Stephen Lee Garden
at Caesars 1989

My first cruise, on
Canberra, 1989

1989 Canberra with
Chris North & Nicola,
Stephen Lee Garden,
Phil Raymond
& Hughie Taylor

Me & Hughie Taylor playing
golf in Montego Bay 1989

My first Cruise Director,
Matthew, on Canberra, 1989

157

Canberra 1989 with the show singers,
Nick Taggart and Mark Inscoe

Winning the Best Comedian Award in Jersey 1989

The Class of '89, Caesars Palace

The fabulous Roger Bara Band, Caesars Palace

Me and Stuart Gillies at the
Palace 1990

Me and Pat Mooney at Caesars
Palace 1990

Me and Gary Bushel in 1990,
'Bushel on the Box'

Caesars Palace 1991 with
Pat Mooney & Scott Paige

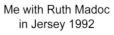

Me with Ruth Madoc
in Jersey 1992

160

Chapter Twenty-Seven

New Beginnings

I became a patron of the Children Say Charity which raised money for children born with hearing impairments who needed cochlear implants.

A lot of money was needed to pay for each operation and once a year at the Wentworth Golf Club a golf day and variety show was organised by the chief patron, Mary Nicklen and her many helpers. The Grand Hall at Wentworth was host to many fine artists and stars. A great day's golf was followed by a fabulous night of entertainment which raised thousands of pounds for this wonderful cause.

A good friend of mine, Chris Gosling, or Goz as he is affectionately known, best mates with Shane, wanted to play the golf and I suggested that he did ten minutes in the show. Without hesitation he jumped at it and I gave him a few funnies and he went down well. Enthusiasm is everything. Well done Goz!

I wanted to join Wentworth Golf Club. There's a forty-five year waiting list. Bing Crosby has just got in!

I thought, shall I join Wentworth or buy a villa in Marbella!

My two favourite shots in golf are the practice swing and the conceded putt!

Golf is a bit like sex. You always think that you can do better next time!

Give me a set of clubs, some fresh air and a gorgeous girl and you can stick your clubs up your arse!

Sadly, Mary is no longer with us, she passed away in 2011. She did a fantastic job and was a remarkable woman.

She is very sadly missed.

An audition for a remake of TV's Who Do You Do came to nothing but taking the children to see Shane in Grease in London made up for it. He was great and we could see then that he was well on his way. His career has gone from strength to strength. Nice one Reg!

A few nights at the Tandoori Indian Restaurant at Thundersley in Essex provided some light relief, quite a bit in fact!

We gave India back and they gave us their restaurants and take-aways!

An Indian meal. That's what I call fast food!

It goes through me like Lynford Christie! (It was 1994!)

Vindaloo? Yeh, four times!

I only thought it was hot going in!

The next day you're afraid to cough!

You have to put your toilet rolls in the fridge!

You can't beat a nice spicy gag!

Now was the time that I picked up the keys to my new house. I had been living at no fixed abode for the last five years and it was good to have a permanent base again.
It was also around this time that I met Kirsty, a local Ipswich girl who was bluecoating at the Pontins Centre in Hemsby, Norfolk.

A gig at the Austin Rover Social Club at Longbridge resulted in my beloved Astra 2.0 litre, 16 valve car being stolen. This was becoming a bit of a habit! There were cameras everywhere in the car park so it was obviously an inside job! Thieving bastards. I loved that car and had bought it in Jersey in 1990, it was cheaper there with no VAT!

International Artistes gave me a few more adult comedy weekends at Bognor and Minehead which, believe it or not, I really enjoyed. They were hard, hostile audiences who had a few bevvies inside them but I could go in stronger and be more aggressive which I liked to do occasionally. Getting things off your chest is good for you, especially in a comedic way. I went for it on this occasion, making fun of the bad things that go on around us. Spicing the subject matter up can sometimes emphasise the comedy!
The Midlands was always a firm favourite for me to work, except Longbridge! Apart from the net weeks (when a set fee is paid for a certain number of shows

162

in a week), the Kingfisher Country Club became a regular haunt which was just on the outskirts of Wolverhampton. Thinking back, working all over the country helped me to pick up the dialects and accents that I use in my act today, which are exaggerated for the comedy effect of course!

A man goes into a shop in Wolverhampton to buy some 'seventies' clothes. He gets some flared trousers and a flowered shirt and the assistant asks, "Would you like a Kipper Tie?" He replies, "Yes please.....milk, no sugar!"

A couple were in a taxi on their way to Southampton from the Midlands and the wife is hard of hearing. The taxi driver asks, "Where are you going?" The husband replies, "We are picking up the cruise ship in Southampton." The wife says, "What did he say?" He said, "He wants to know where we're going." The driver then asks, "Where are you from?" He says, "We're from Birmingham." She says, "What did he say?" "He wants to know where we're from." The driver said, "I went there once and met the ugliest woman in the world." She asks, "What did he say?" The husband says, "He knows ya!"

The privately owned Vauxhall Holiday Park at Great Yarmouth had become a firm favourite. It was always a late show which meant that I could open up a bit more.

As well as the major holiday centres there was another mini season in Jersey including my own Comedy Madhouse at the Royal Hotel in St. Helier.

With the Warners circuit in full flow and now Potters at Hopton becoming a regular venue, the gigs were coming in thick and fast. Potters is a fabulous place to work. It has developed and expanded over the years and I look forward to working there every time. The theatre, the staff and audiences always guarantee a wonderful evening.

As I say, diversity is everything and I was covering the entire spectrum even working at the Gala Bingo Halls! I performed at one in Leicester and what an eye-opener it was! Different to say the least and what a challenge, eyes down, here's your first joke:

I'd like ninety people up to check the balls!

There's three balls missing so we're only playing for single lines!

Your first number is this one... good luck!

Remember this was twenty years ago........

Chinese Bingo Caller:
All the three's...Cantonese!
Chicken Chow Mien... number ten!

Indian Bingo Caller:
Poppadom Naan...number one!
Three and six......Bombay Mix!

Jewish Bingo Caller:
All the fives, fifty-five.....to you, fifty-four!

Geordie Bingo Caller:
Y I 5 0

Norfolk Bingo Caller:
6 and 2........8

The year began with a holiday as it had been a long time since I had a proper break with no work, and it was not going to be a busman's holiday.

I took Claire and James to Florida for two weeks. We had a fantastic time and stayed in a villa that Shane had timeshared. We visited Disney World, Cocoa Beach, Typhoon Lagoon, Tampa, you name it we did it! It was great to get away and no driving on the M25! More importantly, it was so good to spend quality time with my kids.

The year was busier than ever even though there was no cruising in the book but Pontins, Butlins, Warners, clubs, pubs, hotels, Stag and Hen nights were still in great abundance. Other gigs added to the regulars included; Newmarket Celebrities (newly named), The Starlight Rooms at Enfield, Boots'n'Laces at Southend and Chigwell Police Club. These were really nice intimate cabaret Venues and I wonder if they are still having live entertainment?

I performed at my local one thousand, five hundred seater Regent Theatre in Ipswich for a charity night to raise money for the Dunblane tragedy. A worthy cause indeed and playing at home made it extra special.

Next was a summer show at Pontins, Pakefield at Lowerstoft, with Kirsty as the female vocalist, three dancers and a backing duo. It was fun and I did enjoy producing this spectacular! Hark at me, Andrew Lloyd Zany!

164

In November I did my first cruise for four years, not on P&O, but the Thomson Sapphire. My son James joined me and unfortunately he got food poisoning we think and was laid up for three days. It was nice to get my foot in the door with a new company and I always enjoy working for Thomson. To cheer my boy up from his laid back cruise I took him to the Theatre of Dreams at Old Trafford as he is a big Manchester United fan. It was a European Cup night and they beat Juventus 3-2. Only a few months earlier they had beaten our home team Ipswich 9-0! So went the gag:

When do they kick off.......every ten minutes!

I saw the year out with a week at the Kingfisher Country Club, gigs for the three main holiday companies and a show that stands out for me in Biggleswade at a Women's Institute evening. The ladies insisted that I had to keep it clean. You do surprise me!

Two ladies in a car, "Agnes, you've just gone through a red light! Agnes, you've just gone through another red light! Agnes, that's another red light you've gone through!" Agnes replied, "Am I driving?"

An old fella is lost in a shopping centre and can't find his wife. I said to him, "See that very attractive blonde lady over there? Start talking to her and your wife will soon turn up!"

I had now been single for nearly six years and my divorce from Pauline was finally through. James and I were always close, he was a bit younger when his mum and I separated, but there had been some distance between Claire and I since the split. I could understand that, so when I wasn't away working I would always try my hardest to see them both.

Eventually we came round to finding ourselves again. It was not easy for Claire at the time but today our relationship could not be better and we could not be closer.

Communication is everything. In the past I used to hate the time I spent away from them but now they are all grown up I feel that they understand the situation a bit more and that I had to be away sometimes for my work. It wasn't easy for any of us.

I love my children unconditionally and would do anything for them. I also have my two grandchildren, Matilda and Toby, here as well. I am such a proud dad and pops.

Chapter Twenty-Eight

Fighting for Laughs

It was around this time that I recorded one of my comedy shows. I filmed and produced my first video for an invited audience. The routine where I parodied the song Diana with Prince Charles and Lady Di was taken out. The tragic death of Lady Diana meant that the routine was instantly removed from my act.

The Children Say charity still had its annual get together and it was always a stand out day in my calendar. Working many venues over and over again made me realise that I had to keep adding and improving material to my repertoire. Many people could see me several times over the years so updating the content of my act was essential.

There was a fab evening with the Welsh funny man, Max Boyce at the Princess Theatre in Hunstanton and then a bizarre gig at the Marriot Hotel in Bristol for the Transport Managers Club Annual Boxing Dinner. The fee was quite exceptional, the most I had ever been paid and I was soon to realise why! There are times now and then when you really have to use all the experience gained from previous years when the going gets tough! The tough get going!

It was an 11.15 pm spot, all men in a big function room with a boxing ring. Before I went on there were three fights amongst the punters outside of the ring!

Anyway, I got in, ducked and dived and pulled no punches! I used all of my boxing experience from my earlier days when I was seven years old!

The year ended with an eighteen night run at the Mayfair Suite in Seaton Carew, Hartlepool, staying in pro digs. The production show went well, a friendly company but I did miss my home comforts. I felt a long way from home. You can take the boy out of Ipswich……

Can I have burnt bacon, hard eggs and cold beans. I'm homesick!

I took Claire and James back to Florida for another well earnt holiday. My good buddy Dain Cordean, a very talented comedy magician, came as well and we all had a fab two weeks. We work together often on land and at sea and we still talk about that holiday today. I thought it might be the last one for a while as P&O had come calling again. I had served my time!

I went on the *Oriana* for a month from Sydney to Hong Kong, it was a wonderful voyage and all went well. It was a nice return to the high seas and there was no sign of Mick Jagger and those big lips!

I was at Immigration at Sydney Airport and the Immigration Officer asked, "Do you have a prison record?" I replied, "Why, do you still need one?!"

The Aussies seem to answer a question with a question;

What's your favourite colour blue?

What do you do for a hobby sport?

What do you do for a living digger?

In those early days of cruising people would say, "Look, land!" Then a few years later, "Look, I've got a signal on my mobile!" In today's world most ships have a mobile satellite signal so there is contact with the outside world 24/7, but at a cost!

Then followed another month on the *Arcadia*, working with the likes of Mike Doyle, Gary Lovini, Tricia Dusky and Bobby Crush all great people and fabulous acts. I was back with a bang and had a lot more fresher and better material so having to perform two different slots was not a problem. I really enjoyed it on there and the Palladium Theatre and Horizon Lounge were great venues. The ship later became the Ocean Village.

Passengers travel for hours getting to the ship and often get up in the middle of the night to set off. They finally get to the gangway, tired and weary after their long journey and what happens? They take your photograph! Now it matches your passport!

A passenger was heard to say whilst looking at the photo board, "How do I know which one is mine?" Then came the sarcastic reply, "Your cabin number is on the back!"

Three elderly ladies are on deck and the first one said, "It's windy." The second lady replied, "No, I think it's Thursday." The third one said, "So am I, let's have a cup of tea!"

167

Whilst on the Arcadia one elderly lady said, "It's not this windy on the Oriana!"

I left cruising for the summer and concentrated on home soil, the usual major holiday centres and two nights a week in Jersey, my second home!

In October I went back on the *Arcadia* for a six week spell sailing to the Caribbean and back with a great company and a luvley Cruise Director called Neil Oliver. Neil had been the dance instructor on the *Canberra* when I first started sailing and now less than ten years later he had worked his way up to Cruise Director. We have sailed together many times and he is the perfect host and such fun to cruise with. It is always a pleasure to work with Neil and other fellow Cruise Directors whom I have worked with many times over the years on P&O; Hughie Taylor, Ian Fraser, Johnny Bartrum, Nigel Travis, Leon de St Croix, Christine Noble, Natalie Milverton, Elaine Coles and many others too numerous to mention. I went to Hughie's wedding to the lovely Dee the day after I went to Shane's second wedding.

The other artistes on this particular cruise were, Gerard Kenny, Gary Lovini, Susannah Jupp and Jon Wilson who are all really friendly and very talented. This helped enormously with being away for such a long time. I love the Caribbean and have been back there on numerous occasions.

It was eighty degrees in the shade. It was so hot I had to go and sit in the sun! You could tell it was really hot, some of the older ladies had their cardigans unbuttoned!

One elderly lady on deck went topless, then took her bottom set out!

I came out of the swimming pool in my Speedos and I could see all the ladies mentally dressing me!

Between cruises I would continue with the usual gigs and one-offs, Hanbury Manor for a Leukaemia Foundation Charity, the Butlins Grand in Bayswater and then Hunters' Meet Restaurant in Hatfield Heath, Hertfordshire. This was a very intimate dinner dance and cabaret establishment and I still work there today. It is one of the very few venues that have survived and Brendan, another perfect host, loves his comedy.

A weird one-off at the Rembrandt Hotel in Weymouth stands out. I was in one room and the audience were in another.....work that one out? I didn't hang about to ask why?!

In the last fifteen years or so cruising has featured prominently in my work probably due to the demise of venues and summer seasons. With new ships on the horizon all the time and top quality acts working on these luxury liners it became so important to keep writing better and more suitable material if I was to be on a par or better than these very talented performers.

With no cruising or work in January I went back to Florida again and this was sadly to be the last time to date.

Trying to find a happy medium between cruising and the one nighters was my target. Performing on ships is quality work, some theatres hold up to 1,500 passengers with orchestras to die for.

Cruising can vary from the freestyle and lower budget companies to the more exclusive end of the market.

Either way, entertainment on ships is more important and prevalent than ever. You have to be on top of your game though and it is survival of the fittest someone once told me.

February, March and April were busy months back on P&O with one stint on the *Arcadia* from the Seychelles to Istanbul. Apart from earning a decent living and getting job satisfaction I was seeing an awful lot of the world!

I then went back on P&O's smallest vessel, the *Victoria*, which had a more intimate feel to it with the luxurious International Lounge and the late night venue, the Carib Club.

The passengers were mainly British on the ships which sailed out of the UK, but on the world cruises there would be many different nationalities as well. The Brits, and more often the English, have their funny ways and I would exaggerate and incorporate these into my act;

Who walks down the corridor and when they see a cabin door open, look in to see if it's bigger and better than yours!

A lady said to me, "Your cabin is small." I said, "We're in the lift love!"

She's lost all her husband's clothes, she thought her porthole was a washer/dryer!

On all cruises everyone on board has to do a safety drill, it's the law.

I would be really scared if I saw water coming down the stairs. You want to be scared if you see water coming UP the stairs!

The summer yet again saw me do another four shows in Jersey over two nights, you can probably gather now that I really enjoyed doing those shows! A medley of Havens followed; Wild Duck, California Cliffs, Seashore and Cherry Tree which kept my feet firmly on the ground. I then went to Blackpool again, or should I say Lytham St. Annes, to attend the wedding of my good mate Gary Lovini to the lovely Emma...it was a fab day. Gary, an extremely talented violinist, is one of the top artistes you'll find on any cruise liner. A class act!

In October of that year I began cruising for Fred Olsen. It was on a very small ship called the *Black Prince*, only 10,000 tonnes, but size isn't everything, am I right ladies?!

The booker, Roger Lee had been to Potters at Hopton to see me work. He was suitably impressed and my Fred Olsen career began.

It was a very friendly ship, it is out of commission now, and that cruise with Colin Fingers Henry, Wayne Denton and Nina Dusky was really enjoyable. They were very talented acts and fun to cruise with. The passengers were the more mature students, shall we say.

Black Prince is a very old ship. The portholes are bi-focal!

When they said it was going to be in the nineties, I thought they meant the weather!

We had the midnight buffet at half past six!

After three days we had a riot. They ran out of prunes!

170

The Fred Olsen Suite on deck nine is right at the top of the ship. You can never get to see him though, it has F.O. on the door!

It also helps having the head office of Fred Olsen only ten minutes from my doorstep in Ipswich!

The following month I spent a lovely week on a small Greek ship called the *Bolero* for Festival Cruises, Louis Lines. It was one of a few smaller companies I enjoyed working for. They are very small and intimate but very friendly, down to earth and great for comedy.

As 2000 drew closer and closer everything seemed to be ticking along nicely but somewhere inside I was hoping something might happen to give me that extra profile to go on and do even bigger and better things. What's the old saying - being in the right place at the right time.

It was now twenty years since I had turned pro. I'd had my moments and special times, the work was coming in and I still had the passion after all this time. Deep down I was confident that I could raise my game and move up to another level.

Chapter Twenty-Nine

The New Millennium

On the eve of the Millennium I did a cabaret at one of my favourite venues, the Orwell Hotel in Felixstowe, just a ten minute journey from my home. I have played there many times at this prestigious venue! It is run by my very good friend, Lord Richard Furneaux Cattermole, and in our case we certainly mix business with pleasure! I went to his and his lovely wife Judy's wedding at the Orwell a few years ago and a wonderful time was had by all.

I spent the first few weeks of the new Millennium on two world cruise legs, Southampton to San Francisco on *Oriana* and Aquaba to Singapore on *Victoria*. Not a bad way to start the year 2000! The first leg of a world cruise is usually the best, for obvious reasons as the passengers are raring to go, and it turned out that way as I was sharing the bill with my very good friend Stuart Gilles, Carlo Paul Santana, a fabulous cabaret singer, and Peter Carrie of Phantom of the Opera fame. Sharing the comedy with me was the inimitable Tom O'Connor.

A few weeks later I was on the *Arcadia* again and had a great experience with the legendary BBC's Formula One commentator, Murray Walker. We did a late night crew show together, I did the funnies and then we set up a Scalextric track and Murray commentated on the races. It was great fun and a moment to savour. Not many people can say they have played Scalextric with Murray Walker!

My cruising work was now in full swing but once again I found that I became a victim of my own success in some ways. People would tell me how lucky I was and how wonderful it must be to be cruising the high seas and getting paid for it. Don't get me wrong, I love the performing side of cruising but I do not particularly like being away from home. I'm a home-boy at heart. Some people find it hard to understand but we are not talking about a two week annual holiday abroad, its twenty-odd weeks away and I would get very homesick.

It is easier however when you have other performers on the ship with you who you can socialise with but the worse scenario for me is spending too much time on my own. It was hard for me to turn down this good quality work though and do less rewarding bread and butter stuff, driving miles and miles to earn a living.

A certain Mr Simon Cowell likes to knock artistes who choose to perform on cruise ships. What does he know?! I have worked with many great acts over the years and so much talent. The likes that one can see on Britain's Got Talent do not come anywhere close to those that work off shore. BGT is all about watching the very best or the very worst, don't knock what you haven't seen Mr Cowell. I'm rambling and I'm not even dressed for it!

The cruising market was going from strength to strength and becoming more and more affordable to the average household. As the ships get bigger, so do the budgets, and they now have more acts as the rotation of talent is essential. Also, it can be quite intimidating sometimes travelling to a ship in different countries around the world, tiny islands and places in the middle of nowhere. There is not much danger aboard ships, except for the odd Force 12 now and again but getting to and from ships can sometimes have its moments!

A lot of time is spent on planes or at airports:

I spent four days in the Canaries. Two days half-board and the other two I was a bit happier!

At Check In I asked for one case to go to Tenerife, one to Lanzarote and other to Cardiff. She said, "We can't do that Sir." I said, "You did last time!"

One case had a week in Tenerife, the other had a week in Lanzarote!

The stewardess had no sense of humour. She asked, "Tea or coffee Sir?" I replied, "I give up, what is it?!"

An older lady asked me, "Where's the best place to sit young man?" I said, "In the toilet, save you getting up!"

I asked her, "Do you want to sit near the window?" She replied: "No, I've just had my hair done!"

On the *Victoria* cruise with me was Colin Areety and two handicraft ladies who were due to provide the craft lessons on board. We were travelling together and had to pick up the ship in *Aquaba*. We flew to Oman, stayed overnight and then travelled on to Amman, not arriving until after midnight. We could see the ship in the distance but were taken to what seemed like some derelict buildings to sort out immigration. We left Agnes and her friend (the two handicraft ladies) in the van whilst Colin and I were taken to be interrogated. All sorts of things run through your mind in these situations. What if we were taken hostage? How much would they get for a comedian, singer and two handicraft ladies? The mind boggles!

Colin was a lovely gentle Nat King Cole type singer but a hard man from the back streets of Liverpool and even he said the situation was a little scary. The local gestapo eventually realised that we were no danger to them or their country. I had felt that my middle eastern gags would not work in our favour or ease the tension!

An Arab drug dealer... abadabadis!

I went to KFC.... Kentucky Fried Camel!

The second largest mosque in the world is in Agadir....the largest one is in Peckham!

If you commit adultery over there, you get stoned. Over here, it's the other way round!

With Fred Olsen continuing to book me and having now completed over ten years with P&O, another line was now offering me work, Airtours. They had the *Sunbird*, *Sundream* and *Carousel*, the latter were two small ships, and very intimate with the audiences once again very much down to earth and up close and personal so contact was usually immediate. I always think that the closer they are to you the better unless they want to fight, then distance is essential!

My first cruise on *Sunbird* never actually took place! I arrived in Tenerife to pick up the vessel but no luggage arrived! I met with the Captain, Philip Rentall, who loved his comedy, and the Cruise Director, Roy Yates. The decision was made for me not to sail. I stayed for two nights in a hotel, my luggage arrived and then I flew home! This would never happen today, I would have to get on and do the cruise and make do, grabbing clothes from all and sundry!

I spent three great years with Airtours, met lots of lovely acts and the passengers were always up for a laugh.

I met the wife on a cruise ship. I said, "What are YOU doing here?!"

I'm so tired. My Cabin Steward got me up at half past six this morning, that's the last time I sleep with her!

I lay on my bed at five o'clock this evening, completely naked, and she came in … finally!

She said, "Can I turn your bed down?" I said, "You might as well, everybody else on here has!"

Gladys was on the toilet in her cabin and she flushed the loo before she got up and is now suctioned on there! (The plumbing is a Hoover system on ships!) She said, "Arfur, call the plumber, I can't get off, I'm stuck in the loo!" Whilst the plumber is on the way to the cabin, Gladys says to her husband, "You'll have to preserve my dignity, get your flat cap and put it down there." The plumber comes to the cabin and Arfur asks, "Can you get her off?" The plumber replies, "The wife's ok but the bloke in the hat is a goner!"

There then followed repeat cruises on *Bolero* and the *Black Prince* and a one-off on another very small ship called the *Aussonia*.

The brand new P&O *Aurora* was next, a real luxury liner that I still do today, fifteen years on. I was now getting regular work with P&O, Olsen and Airtours and felt well and truly established on the cruising circuit.

For some cruises I would fly out to a foreign port to pick up the ships but a lot of the time I would depart from the UK, usually Southampton or Dover, now and again Harwich. Going south from the mainland along the Channel, through the Bay of Biscay then down the Atlantic can sometimes be a little bit, shall we say, rock 'n'roll!

We are just going through the Bay of 'Sickbay'!

You can tell those that are drunk –they are the ones that are walking straight!

The Bay of Biscay dance: slow, slow, quick, quick, slow!

I like to go a different colour on holiday... but not green!

"Doctor, what is the best cure for sea sickness?" "Land!"

The Doctor said, "I will give you an injection." I asked, "Will it hurt?" He replied, "Only when you get the bill!"

It can be so expensive to see the Doctor on board a ship, there's no NHS!

I went for a check-up and asked, "Where shall I put my clothes?" "Over there, next to mine!"

When you have a check-up on a ship he holds your wallet and says 'cough'!

I got a bad chest. I had to cough up £50!

There's a nasty bug going around. I opened my cabin door and there stood a six foot cockroach!

Since that time on the *Aurora* there have been many more ships and it seemed that the cruising market was on the up and up and would become the major earner for me, but I was still trying to find the quality gigs back home.

Although I was kept busy on the cruises it's fair to say that more time was spent on land gigging, but mainly in the south.

Special nights were still coming along now and again, a sportsman's dinner for Ipswich Town Football Club, my home team who I have supported man and boy. This gave me the opportunity to have a pop at them and take the mickey if the boys weren't doing too well. They always took it in good spirits to be fair to them. If we were doing ok, I would switch to our rivals, Norwich City. That would be even better and more appreciated – obviously. It is always funnier in a Norfolk accent anyway.

The 'Player of the Year' was a rollover!

Golden goal... November!

They plan to be in the Premiership for three seasons. Autumn, Winter and Spring!

A couple named their baby after the team. They called it.. Absolute F***ing Disgrace!

A supporter's dying wish was to be stuffed and put in the stand at Carrow Road (Norwich City). When he passed away they did this and at half time he went home!

Warner's Holiday Parks were still in full flow, we used to say they were a cruising audience on land, very receptive and the venues are great. We would travel as far as Torquay, Weymouth, Devon, Somerset and even North Wales! It was always a satisfying night at Warners. Sadly over the last few years they have tightened their belts and cut the budgets somewhat.

Family rooms made it much harder to enjoy the work especially for stand-up. It is never nice to work in venues where the children outnumber the mums and dads. Call me old fashioned! Concentration levels are somewhat distracted for them and expecting young kids to be quiet for forty minutes or so is not going to happen. No way Pedro!

In early 2001 I was cruising on Fred Olsen's *Black Watch*, it was a leg of the South American tour from Punta Arenas up to Lima in Peru. I have been to a few remote places in my career which led me to say to some passengers once, "Only two people have been here before, Christopher Columbus and Fred Olsen!"
The cruise in question was a superb one geographically and we sailed up the western coast of Chile. The Chilean Fjords are absolutely amazing.
Before we flew home from Lima there was time to buy one or two souvenirs

including a handmade wooden Llama from a craft market. Once again, you had to be there to sample the ambience of the place.

Then something worrying happened. Before my first gig on this cruise I went to the loo and afterwards noticed quite a lot of blood in the toilet. Having never seen this before it was a bit of a shock to say the least and I got an awful feeling. I didn't remember eating that much beetroot!

I can remember watching Bob Monkhouse on Parkinson once. He knew he was dying of prostate cancer and his way of dealing with it was through humour.

I was passing the undertakers the other day and saw a sign; Bob Monkhouse – coming soon!

I applaud him for that, others might not find it so funny, but hey, every man to his own.

He was one of my favourite stand-ups, with great original material and he was unsurpassed when it came to game shows. He was the governor.

Getting back to the bottom of the matter, I went to see the doctor and he arranged for me to have an endoscopy at my local hospital to check mainly, I assumed, for bowel cancer.

I was the first patient to go in that day and with my backless gown, paper shorts and black socks I found myself lying quite nervously there on the table with my arse protruding out and into the air! Like someone was going to park their bicycle there!

With the sister at that end and a nurse holding my hand at the better looking end and the doctor across the room reading the Sun newspaper, all I could think of at the time was the funny side of the procedure. A bit like Mr. Monkhouse but in a more graphic way. I cannot imagine anyone performing the following routine on stage unless they had actually been through it!

With the doctor being so far away I was thinking that he was going to take a run up!

The sister remarked that I had a lovely butt. I replied that it was a shame it had a crack in it!

I was not relishing the thought of a camera going up there!

The sister said, "Finger going in." To which I replied, "Shouldn't we go for a drink and a meal first!"

Through all this embarrassment I actually thought of a joke! While the doctor was carrying out this excerpt from Journey Into The Unknown, he asked me quite sincerely;

"Am I the only Doctor you are seeing?" To which I replied coyly, "Oh, yes Doctor, no need to worry, you're the only one!"

What a job, start off at the bottom and stay there!

A short time ago I had to go for a prostate check.

I was going to have my prostate checked but I couldn't be arsed!

And look where God put it, what a sense of humour he has!

Anyway, the doctor gave me the thumbs up!

I was lying there once again and the doctor said, "I can see where your hair went!"

Rewind backwards a few lines, I am very glad to say that the outcome was negative. What a relief!

A Caribbean cruise on P&O's *Victoria* and a week on *Sunbird*, this time with my luggage, was to follow that South American leg.

On a brighter note, my partner Kirsty and I had been in our new house only two months and I thought it would be a nice touch to bring a memento home from that South American Cruise. So I gave her the handmade wooden Llama from the craft market in Lima, Peru. I don't think she liked it because when I came home from my next cruise on *Victoria*, the Llama was hanging by a rope from a light fitting!

Sometimes you have to be there to appreciate the local culture, Lima that is! If the truth be known it didn't have any diamonds on it!

I bought some of that perfume home for her, what was it called? Tester! She wasn't happy!

I had a one night stand and it all went wrong. I've been married for three years now!

Love has a ring to it... suffering!

My wife has sinus trouble. Sinus a cheque for this, sinus a cheque for that!

"My wife's an angel." "You're lucky, mine's still living!"

Take away her attractive looks and stunning body and what have you got? My missus!

Do you like women with long greasy hair, big saggy boobs and really fat legs? No you don't? Then why are you sleeping with my missus?

I forgave Kirsty for electrocuting the Llama and in May 2001 we got married. My divorce was not working out!

Chapter Thirty

Dead Funny!

The first six months of 2001 turned out to be a busy one with another three cruises on Fred Olsen's *Black Prince* and P&O's *Aurora* and *Oriana*.

The world cruise audiences are usually made up of the more senior generation, or recycled teenagers as they prefer to be called! They were the ones who had the money saved or could afford to go on a worldie! Though things have changed somewhat in today's economic climate.

Your pension doesn't go far does it? Sydney, Cape Town, New York...!

It was often the case that on most world cruises one or two of the passengers would not come back, but what a way to go, on a luxury cruise. As a widow once said:

".....it's what he would have wanted."

In the summer of this year I had a very strange experience at the Vauxhall Holiday Park in Great Yarmouth, a venue I had performed at on a regular basis.

I was due to follow the talent show winner, a Scottish singer, a man in his late fifties. He collected the first prize and then minutes later he collapsed; he had a massive heart attack and was pronounced dead at the scene. He was taken away from the lounge by the paramedics and you can guess what the atmosphere was like in the room. It was very sad, we were all stunned and I was all ready to go on stage but now thought it would be inappropriate and disrespectful. I've heard of being dead funny but Bernie, our lovable M.C. actually went out and asked the audience if they thought it would be ok to put the comic on. The response was a unanimous, 'Yes'! Thinking back, it wasn't so much as what to say but more what not to say. I didn't want to be the second person dying on the night.

Luckily I did alright and there have been many occasions, not quite like this one, when experience counts for everything.

I rang up the doctors to make an appointment and they said, "Is it an emergency?" I replied, "Well, I have a Priest at the bottom of the bed!"

I sat in the waiting room so long I caught three other diseases!

I went to see the doctor last week. I've had a problem with my ears and I've heard nothing from him!

He found some baked beans in one ear and a sausage in the other. He said, "You're not eating properly!"

I said, "I've got Amnesia," He said, "Forget it, don't worry about it!"

I said, "I'm an Insomniac." He replied, "Don't lose any sleep over it!"

I said, "I'm a Kleptomaniac." He replied, "Are you taking anything for it?"

He told me I suffered from Hypochondria. I said, "Oh no, not that as well!"

In August of 2001 Fred Olsen launched their new ship the *Braemar*. It was docked in Dover and I went down to do two nights to a corporate audience. This included, Fred Olsen staff, their guests, showbiz agents, travel agents and such like, so it was not your normal cruising audience. All went well and I shared the bill with a BeatlesTribute Band. Going well turned out to be a feather in my cap as lots of openings came along and I have cruised on *Braemar* many times up to the present day.

Then that fateful day came along, 9/11. I am sure that everybody remembers where they were on that day, I know I do.

The evening before I had gigged at a regular holiday centre at Lyme Bay in Seaton, Devon and it was always a great place to work. It was really good to see my old friends Scott and Jo whom I had great times with at Plemont Bay in Jersey, plus a good backing band and dancers to match. It was always a fab time here with the gang and I usually stayed the night at Lyme Bay because it was a long drive back to Ipswich.

The next day I was due to perform at a corporate function at the Alton Towers Hotel in Staffordshire. I had never been there before and have not been back since. The journey was very long, up the M5, on to the M6 and then on to the venue. I remember at almost 2pm that afternoon the news came over the radio saying that an aircraft had hit one of the Twin Towers, and that there had been some sort of accident, then another plane hit, then ......stunned amazement.

I can remember booking into the hotel and someone from the Company I was working for told me to be at the meal for 7.30pm. It was going to be an after dinner performance to only a small number of people. I went down at 7.30pm and someone gave me the cheque and then almost immediately after that I was told that I would not be doing the show because the company had offices in the Twin Towers and they didn't think it was appropriate for me to perform.

After what had happened a few weeks earlier at Great Yarmouth when the talent show winner suddenly passed away, at least this time total respect was shown. I went back to my room and watched the events of that day unravel on the TV. It was horrendous.

It was a strange night and I drove home the next day still in a daze. What a world that we live in when this atrocity could have even been imaginable.

Further cruises on *Sundream*, *Aussonia*, *Black Watch* and *Black Prince* saw me complete fifteen weeks at sea that year. Corporate functions were a nice change from the bread and butter gigs. We did a golf day for Mercedes Benz, a sponsors dinner at the Spurs v Middlesborough game at White Hart Lane and a Children In Need fund raising event at my local 1,500 seater Regent Theatre. This was followed by the annual Children Say golf day at Wentworth. This was always a dream day, playing golf on the west course straight after the World Matchplay Championships.

A few months after performing at the inaugural corporate evenings in Dover, I did my first cruise proper on the *Braemar*. It has been a regular since then to the present day so updating my act is essential because of the returning passengers.

I lost my cabin key today. I had a Scout round, but he couldn't find it either!

I said to the lady behind reception last night, "Can you give me a wake-up call?" She said, "You're fifty, single, wear an earring.... get a life!"

I went to the hairdressers, she said, "You're losing your hair." I said, "I haven't, it's in a bag in my cabin!"

I don't like hairdressers, they talk behind your back!

I said to the fitness girl, "I want to do the Aerobics class." She said, "How flexible are you?" I said, "I can't do Tuesdays!"

I said, "How can I get a body like yours?" She replied, "Swop heads!"

I went for a massage. It was self-service!

I said to the young masseur, "Where have you been all my life?" She said, "Teething!"

"I'd like a full body massage please." She said, "Take all your clothes off young man." So I did and she said, "Put them back on again old fella!"

There followed a very up market corporate function at the Penny Hill Hotel in Bagshot, Surrey, which is next to Ascot, very lah de dah......

They have a Kentucky Fried Pheasant in Bagshot!

If a lady has bags under her eyes, they're probably Gucci!

I saw a homeless person in Bagshot. He said, "Have you got five pounds for a croissant!"

He asked, "Any spare change?" I replied, "I've left it in my spare wallet!"

He said, "I've not eaten for four days." I replied, "I wish I had your will power!"

I met a homeless person from England in Tenerife and asked, "What are you doing here?" He said, "I'm on my holidays!"

The company was called Motivation and the evening consisted of a buffet for forty people, then me for thirty minutes. It was a dream gig, simply spiffing! The clients were rather well to do and the venue was very salubrious which made it perfect for the material I used. I do like a challenge – especially when I win!

The say that bad luck comes in threes. Well after the talent show winner dying in Yarmouth and 9/11, what else could there be? I know, a wake!

184

Chapter Thirty-One

The Good, The Bad and the Ugly

A local yachtsman, Steve Hall, sadly passed away and one of his final wishes was to have me do a comedy show at his wake straight after the funeral. It was at the clubhouse in Woolverstone Marina near Ipswich and a four piece band were banging out music, then they had a minute's silence, then me!

Another strange situation but the thirty minute slot went well and I used him and the situation in my performance. It made it more personal and I know Steve would have loved it. He was a super guy.

I went to three funerals last week, I'm not even a morning person!

I had a bit of bad luck at one of them, I caught the wreath!

The fella had passed away; he got hit on the head with a tennis ball. Still, it was a good service!

The pallbearers came into the cemetery with the coffin, walked round for ten minutes and then walked out of the cemetery with the coffin. I thought to myself, they've lost the plot!

I wish I could do more wakes! A celebration of one's life rather than a mourning. I don't do many weddings either, comedy shows that is, and no, a wedding is not a funeral where you smell your own flowers!

Another upmarket corporate event at Surrey Cricket Club was followed by a fun night at Lowestoft Police Station. It was always a guaranteed cracker of a night – a lock in!

You can poke fun at the Police and they can take it, thankfully, but only when they are off duty. A Police routine will always be topical and fit the bill, ha ha!

He pulled me over and put his head through the window – and they're forty quid a time!

He said, "Are you the driver of this vehicle Sir?" I said, "It is automatic but I have to sit here!"

"Have you read the Highway Code?" I said, "No, I'm waiting for the film to come out!"

"Do you know how fast you were going?" I said, "The same as you!"

He asked, "What's all the hurry?" I replied, "My wife ran off with a Policeman a while ago and I thought you were bringing her back!"

Whenever you perform for an audience where the majority share the same workplace, you are usually guaranteed a bigger laugh, whether it be the Police, doctors, accountants, builders, lorry drivers, golf days, football dinners and so forth.

Further to working the upmarket corporate functions, I moved up a niche in cruising circles to fly out and pick up the last few days of a world cruise on the six star *Seabourn Sun*. Another challenge was ahead but this one turned out to be a somewhat sour one thanks to an unfriendly Cruise Director! Most of my cruising career to date had been with really friendly Cruise Directors, however, this was one of those rare moments. I cannot remember his name which is probably a good thing, but let me just say that he made me feel as welcome as a fart in a lift! His opening line to me when we met wasn't very polite and it was painfully obvious that he had had enough comedy to date and did not want any more. Imagine how I felt having travelled half way around the world to get there.

Considering the way he made me feel my show went alright. There were not too many Brits on, a lot of Americans and a few Europeans, but overall my set was warmly received. Even Mr. Tosser came back stage and complimented me.

I have never seen him since and I hope I never do. Life is too short to waste on people who are rude and have no respect...See you next Tuesday!

I flew to Rio next to pick up *Aurora* and sailed back to Southampton which was just the tonic after my last forgettable experience. Bonnie Langford was on board with her then baby son and she was lovely – a class act!

I have had the pleasure and fortune to work with many fabulous acts on the seven seas over the years on P&O, including the likes of Bobby Crush, Roy Walker, Gerard Kenny, Tom O'Connor, Allen Stewart, Jeff Stevenson, Stuart Gillies, Gary Lovini, Hilary O'Neil, Iris Williams, Mike Doyle and many, many more.

I've known Doyley for thirty years, man and boy, another top act and it was a special day to see him tie the knot with the lovely Maree.

I have put together many of my own comedy shows in various venues in and around Ipswich. I do get an extra kick in seeing my family, friends and guests really enjoying themselves and having a bloody good night out. They would also be invited to come along and give their support when I was filming a new video or DVD. I was still the boy next door to them – literally!

Why does the next door neighbour's cat do its jobbies in MY garden? I throw stones at it... he's got wise now and he sits in front of my Greenhouse!

My neighbour's have got a vicious Rottweiler and it barks all day long. I'm going to put it in my garden and see how they like it!

The neighbour said, "Don't worry, he won't hurt you, I've had him done, neutered." And there was me thinking he was going to bite me!

Over the years I have produced three videos and three DVD's. I am constantly changing, updating and writing new stuff for this reason as well.

Sailing with Airtours *Sunbird, Sundream* and *Carousel* meant that I performed to a younger clientele which were more family orientated then the more sedate cruising passengers thus allowing for more edgier material when the children were not allowed in.

I'd like to be sick over a baby and see how they like it!

I saw a sign which read, Caution, small children playing. I'm not scared of small children!

They say get a dog not a child – a dog will only ruin your carpet!

You have got to look after your kids though. They decide which care home you're going into!

A fella knocked on the front door and a six year old boy opens it with a cigar in one hand and a can of beer in the other. The man said, "Is your dad in?" And the boy replied, "Does it look like it?!"

The *Braemar* was still full speed ahead –I was part of the family now! Next came Page and Moy's *Ocean Majesty*, another small vessel, so intimate and friendly and every performance was part of a variety show and they made me feel very welcome – unlike Mr Tosser!

Christine Butler, a wonderful, sweet Cruise Director who always made me feel like one of the family was on that ship. We went on to sail together on Fred Olsen and it is always comforting to know that I was going to be working with special people, unlike Mr, yeah I know, you've got the message!

It has now been ten years since I did a full summer season at Caesars Palace in Jersey but along came the chance to do twelve weeks on the *Black Watch*. Six cruises which included three Baltics and three Norways. A long time to be away but Kirsty came on all three Baltics, every other cruise, which softened the blow. A Baltic cruise is always very interesting taking in the capitals; Helsinki, Oslo, Copenhagen, Stockholm, Tallinn, Northern Germany with St Petersburg in Russia being the highlight.

Spending so much time on one ship, a summer season in fact, meant that I got to know the staff and crew very well and I got to feel more at home which was comforting to say the least. With Cruise Directors such as, John Butt, Michael Burke, Gary Nicholson, Ronnie Finch and Alan Tait at the helm, all was well!

A fella asked me, "Which way is it to the pointed end?" I replied, "It's that way Captain!"

A passenger got an invitation to sit at the Captain's table for dinner and he said, "No thanks, I'm not eating with the crew!"

Does anyone know which ports we are sailing to? It's not for me, the Captain has lost the brochure!

In those twelve weeks I worked with some fine acts, Steve Hewlett, a great ventriloquist (now of Britain's Got Talent fame). He's so good that when he talks in his sleep his lips don't move! Andrew Robley, a West End singer and a firm favourite on Fred Olsen was with us as well. The three of us did the whole season together and were joined by guest artistes, Sid Little, Jon Bell and Mel Mellors to name just a few.

The trips to Norway were always interesting especially the days in the Fjords which are so tranquil and so remote. Only a scattering of houses are around the surrounding hills and I cannot imagine living there so far removed from normal life. It is also very expensive to live in Norway like most of Scandinavia.

I'm just off to Tesco's – be back in August!

Apparently the World Hide and Seek champion lives there!

I got mugged here today. £8 for half a lager!

I went for a McDonald's cheeseburger and chips. It was £12 and they called it a Happy Meal!

It was cheaper to eat the money!

With further cruises on the *Ocean Majesty* and Fred Olsen, together with these Summer cruises, meant that I had been afloat for twenty-four weeks that year but the quality one nighters were steadily decreasing and the heady days of the eighties and nineties were well and truly gone.

The quality of work on ships though was there for all to see. A fantastic theatre or cabaret lounge, a full orchestra and the chance to create new material was so inviting. It wasn't easy by any means. Apart from strong quality content the act needed the quantity as well, at least two forty-five minute sets of clean material for all ages!

You meet many people on ships, passengers, cruise staff and acts that you bump into now and again but a lot of the time you are on your own. Fortunately, I have used this time to my advantage as over the last few years I have put pen to paper and written this epic! Killing time on a ship does my head in as I am no good at doing nothing!

A second comedy show in Ipswich was to follow and I was now putting on two a year as the demand was good. I can always get enough quality acts to do the business. The year ended with a variety of shows, a Tarmac golf day, a Charlton Football Club sponsored match and an awkward gig at the Mayflower Chinese Restaurant in Cheltenham. This was a small office function where I thought I would be ok but unfortunately, that was not to be. The audience were office fuddy duddy's and young men out to impress the office girls and the atmosphere was strange to say the least. I thought that my Chinese Restaurant routine would win them over as it had worked in the past, but alas, they seemed to find it somewhat embarrassing! It was groaner time!

The Chinese are very humble, very clever people:

This plate is damp....that's your soup!

The egg is bad.....I only lay the table!

What's the duck like?.....Little bird swim in water!

What's this here, Chicken Tingy?....That is Chicken Ting....chicken done in microwave!

This meal is not fit for a pig... I'll bring you one that is!

After they take your order they swear at you... effin' else!

Unlike before, all is fab when you perform to the Police at their own venue, members at their Golf Clubs, social or working men's clubs where they socialise together, but put some young people out of their little pond and sometimes they feel somewhat inhibited.

This showbiz lark is a great leveller, it wasn't a disaster by any means but I had to work a lot harder than normal. At the end of the day it was an office Christmas party and their main objective was to stuff their faces with as much Chinese food as possible, then get drunk. On top of that there is usually one office comedian who thinks that he will impress the girlies. This particular evening his name was Peter. To be fair I gave him quite a bit of leeway and then came the moment;

Boys and girls, there are a few types of orgasm;
The positive orgasm.......yes, yes, yes.
The negative orgasm.......no, no, no.
The religious orgasm......oh God, oh God, oh God.
Then there's the fake orgasm....oh Peter, oh Peter, oh Peter!

190

They liked that, Peter didn't though. He wasn't much of a spoiler, he'd just had a few too many drinks. I feel a bit sorry for the rest of the audience who are actually wanting to enjoy the show. Compared to the Stag days, this was a drop in the ocean! A much worse heckler was to follow which was at a very uneasy night at RAF Honington in Suffolk.

Most of the shows I do go very well and are so rewarding but now and again a bad one pops up. Once in a blue moon an ugly situation occurs and this was it! All had started so well when at the bar Mr Arsehole decided for some reason that he wanted to be the centre of attention. It was just him as everybody else was enjoying the show. It was a weird moment and he was a big guy so I thought that I would go in gentle;

You're a big fella, if you want to walk about, you walk about.

Do you live in a Greenhouse?!

I'd hate to empty your bedpan!

This seemed to spur him on to thinking that he was part of a double act!

If I want to do a double act, I'll bring my own dummy!

I think this could have been some sort of catalyst. There are good hecklers and bad hecklers. Good ones can get you loads of laughs but unfortunately, this was not one of those occasions.

I tried so hard to do the act but it soon went out of the window, I only wish he had! He was determined to spoil the party and the sad thing was that there was nobody there who was prepared to shut him up. I could only try and do that in a lighthearted way,

If I could afford the wood, I'd board your mouth up!

All those in favour of acupuncture, there's a prick!

He's an advert for safe sex.... wanker!

Were you dropped on your head when you were a baby? No. Well you should have been!

191

The best part of you ran down your dad's leg!

That care in the community is not working!

It was a waste of time. Once again, I felt sorry for all the other guys. The booker was so apologetic but in some masochistic way I enjoyed it!

A week later I was at another venue which could have been difficult. It was a thirtieth anniversary party for a local farmer in this enormous hanger at Elmsett Airfield in Suffolk. It turned out ok mainly because the audience were very nice and also attentive, it certainly overshadowed the verbal diarrhoea from that Mr Knobhead the week before! Sometimes, no matter how funny you are, or think you are, the venue and atmosphere or lack of it can determine how well you go.

Dying on your arse is a horrible experience, but we have all been there. If you haven't then you don't know what you've missed!

A very special corporate gig came along at the Ramada Hotel in Norwich. It was something to do with traffic and the guest of honour was the Chief of the New York Traffic Control Centre or something similar. It was a big room with a big male audience and a big night. Bryan Gunn, the ex-Norwich City goalkeeper, spoke first then me. It ended with a standing ovation, enough said. I don't get too many on the cruises as they haven't got the strength to stand up!

The agent was there watching that night and sometime later the same agent got me another corporate gig in an office complex in Norwich. There wasn't many of them around, about thirty I think, and they were outside the room helping themselves to the buffet. The lady organiser came in and said, "You can start now," to which I replied, "There is nobody in the room!" and she replied, "I'm sure that they will make their way in once you start talking!" From one extreme to another!

It is hard to believe that anybody with any sort of common sense would expect that to be the right thing to do! Some people have no idea and thankfully, I cannot remember ever being put in that kind of pathetic situation at any other time.

The agent was very understanding – NOT! His only fear was losing the client ....agents!

192

Caesars Palace 1992 with
Terry and Mia Carla alongside
Paul Daniels and Debbie McGhee

Me with the boss Dick Ray at
Caesers Palace in 1992

The Show Company
Caesars Palace 1992

Caesars '92, James, Micky,
Carol & Adrian

The Crocodile
Dundee sketch for
Caesars Palace
1992

Me with Paul Daniels
at Caesars 1992

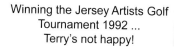

Winning the Jersey Artists Golf
Tournament 1992 ...
Terry's not happy!

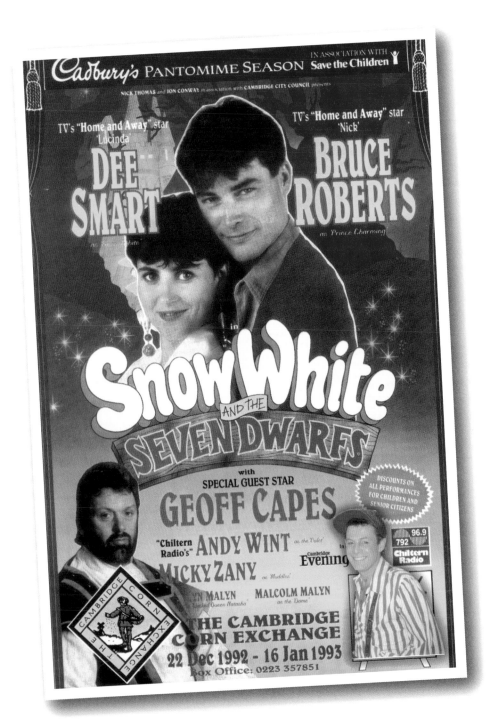

196

The Travelling
Show Company
Nick Thomas
Productions 1993

Scarborough 1993 playing golf,
my son james & Janette Krankie

1992/93 panto with Bruce Roberts
(Home & Away)

Myself & Hilary O'Neil,
Scarborough 1993

197

Sharing the bill
with Billy Pearce

Late night at Butlin's
with Keith Harris & Orville

1993 Scarborough
with Brian Conley

1993 Scarborough with
Roy 'Chubby' Brown

198

1994 on tour with Joe Longthorne

Seeing Shane in Grease
at the Dominion in 1994
with James

Meeting six times major winner Nick Faldo at Wentworth Golf Club in 1994

In Florida 1995
with the kids

Dave Lee Charity Comedy
Show at Canterbury with Billy
Pearce & Bobby Davro

P&O Arcadia 1998 with
Cruise Director Neil Oliver - Luvley!

On Arcadia 1998 with
Gary & Emma Lovini and
Susannah & John Wilson

200

My first
Fred Olsen Cruise
on Black Prince with
Nina Dusky, Wayne
Denton & Colin
'Fingers' Henry

on P&O Arcadia 1998
with Nigel, Doyley
and Bobby Crush

On P&O Oriana
in 1998 with
Gary, Tricia & 'Doyley'

On P&O Victoria 2000
with Gary and Emma Lovini, Lynsey Simon & Colin Areety

On Airtours Sundream 2000
with John Martin and Jonathan Clark

Oriana World Curise in 2000
with Tom O'Connor

On Oriana world
cruise in 2000 with
Stuart Gillies and
Peter Carrie

Me with Mum & Dad & Sister Jan in 2000
at their Golden Wedding Celebration

203

On P&O Aurora 2000 with Paul Emmanuel

On P&O Victoria 2001 being a 'fairy' in the crew show - 'If I were not upon the stage...'

Dec 2001 on Black Watch with the loveable Cruise Director Michael Burke

The Rocky Horror Show - well almost!
Black Watch, 2002.

Black Watch, with my close friends John and Andrea

Gigging with funny guys, Ollie Day and Phil Lowen
and singer Julie Bunn

Tractor Boys Unite - on Braemar with funny boy
Andy Leach

With the gorgous Barbara Windsor
at a Charity Event

With Doyley and Trish
in Cairns, Australia

Me and the Boy with
Jessie 'Kat' Wallace
- Eastenders set!

On Fred Olsen with Helen and Wendy

Aurora 2002 with Robbie Allen,
Roy Barraclough and friend

Chapter Thirty-Two

S.A.G.A.

I took another twenty weeks cruising in 2003, which sounds an awful lot, but it was becoming more sensible to do shorter cruises and more of them. Most cruise companies were realising at this time that performing two different shows over a shorter period and flying the acts in or out was becoming more economical in the long run.

After cruising from Punta Arenas to Lima two years previously I was now travelling from Rio down to the southern tip of South America, also taking in the Falkland Islands as well. It was so good to go back there and see the difference in the last fifteen years or so.

It was at this time that Helen Bennett took over from Roger Lee to become the booker for Fred Olsen cruises. I have had a very good relationship with Helen, Barbara, Louise and all the girls in the office both on a business and social level. The head office is based in Ipswich so it is always nice to call in and have a catch up now and again.

Then followed *Sundream* and *Carousel* again which turned out to be the last cruises for Airtours. They had not only cut out the in house musicians but were asking the cabaret acts to take a pay cut as well. For me it was a time to say goodbye. I was working my way up and I had choices, especially on the cruising circuit. So one company goes and another door opens as they say, and one such company was Saga.

S.A.G.A........Send A Granny Abroad!

The breakthrough came at last through my Airtours agent, Nick Taggart, of Nett UK and his lovely wife Trish, a great singer who I used to work with on P&O and we are very good friends. We had been chasing Saga for over two years and Nick had now managed to get me a booking on the *Saga Rose*.

Some people find it easy to poke fun at Saga because the passengers have to be of a certain age to travel on their ships but they are a very prestigious company and I have been working for them for well over ten years now. It was the Capetown to

209

Mombassa leg of a world cruise which made it no easier. World cruise passengers on any ship, let alone Saga, are well renowned for being tougher. They pay a lot of money and expect top quality. I was very nervous to say the least and well aware that the Saga passengers were again the more mature students of cruising.

The atmosphere was very laid back and it was so important to slow down and be squeaky clean. There were certain gags that I did not do, but which have now become trademark on other cruise lines;

The Ballroom sleeps 400!

I didn't dare put my glass down in case they put their false teeth in it!

The disco is called Slip a Disc!

A lovely elderly gentleman called Arthur was on the Saga Rose, 94 years young, and he was on there looking after his mum and dad!
He was listening to the wall, he saw me and called me over. "Come and have a listen." So I did and I said, "I can't hear anything." He replied, "It's been like that all day!"

He had two wooden legs – but real feet!

I said, "You look a bit miserable Arthur, what's the matter?" He said, "I've got this ten thousand piece jigsaw to do, I can't do it, it's a picture of a chicken." I said, "It's a box of Corn Flakes Arthur!"

I followed Max Bygraves, not literally, I'm not a celebrity stalker! I was a big fan of his going way back to my younger days.

I wanna tell you a story...... Singalongamax.

The show went well beyond my wildest expectations. The Cruise Director, Roy Parkinson, ex *QE2*, said to me, "You are a breath of fresh air." That is all I needed to hear. Max and I, sounds like we were great mates, clashed on only one stock gag.

I was entertaining in a Care Home and I asked one of the residents, "Do you know who I am?" He said, "Ask the matron, she'll tell you!"

I went back on the *Rose* three more times that year and it was sometimes a challenge. I won and I loved it and it was a classy place to be. The line-up was more classical with musicians and lecturers, the light entertainment was in the minority.

On SAGA over the years I have rubbed shoulders with the likes of Esther Rantzen, Edwina Currie, Betty Boothroyd, Sir Bernard Ingham, Jonathan Aitken, Michael Burton and many other excellent speakers and some brilliant classical musicians, too numerous to mention. I do enjoy a bit of classical.........now and again.

Ten years further on and the number of cruise companies I worked for had increased and it was difficult to say no sometimes, but I couldn't do all the work I was being offered or I would have been at sea every day of the year!

For me, if the quality one-nighters were still there the need to go to sea would be much less. Mind you, the attraction or chance to see some of the world on these fantastic ships has great job satisfaction. Also, getting paid for it, would appeal to most people! Sometimes though, the pressure of having to do this all the time can somewhat dampen the attraction especially when I was on my own so much.

I could not imagine being on a cruise for any length of time and not doing well. That indeed would be a very lonely experience!

The year saw two more of my own comedy shows which are always popular and well supported. I do enjoy them and as I don't usually work with many comedy acts on ships, I had to find them from land work or word of mouth. Distance can sometimes be a problem as Ipswich is a bit off the beaten track for some acts, but I always managed to get a good variety of comedy acts and to date all my shows have been very well received. A lot of the punters would not have come back otherwise. The pressure!

I did a couple of shows with Diana Ross and Robbie Williams, tribute acts of course, but still very good. Further cruises on Fred Olsen and P&O made up the rest of my calendar. In between there were the usual suspects of Butlins, Pontins, Haven and Warners and a return to Lowestoft Police Station. Oh no, not more Police jokes!

One more gig here and I'll lose my license!

The Officer said I was speeding. "I've been following you for three miles." I replied, "The answer is still no!"

"You were doing 65 in a 40 limit." I said, "Can you make it 85, I'm trying to sell it?!"

He said, "Anything you say may be taken down and used against you." I said, "Please don't hit me again Officer!"

My dog was on the passenger seat and I smacked him. The Officer said, "That's it, I'm doing you for speeding and cruelty to an animal. What did you hit the dog for?" I said, "The little bugger has just eaten my Tax Disc!"

Everything seemed to be going well, but then I found myself on my own again.

Chapter Thirty-Three

The Break Up

It was 2004 and my marriage to Kirsty was about to break down. It came as somewhat of a surprise to me. There had been moments when all wasn't as it should have been but I suppose, unknowingly, our heads were buried and we hoped that it would be ok and work itself out.

Deep down though if you feel how you should feel for someone, love them unconditionally and trust them one hundred percent, then you don't look for the negatives.

It was easy to find excuses and reasons other than the real one. Kirsty didn't feel the same anymore and neither did I. You fall in love, you fall out of love. We had been together on and off for nine years. We had parted for a while back in 1998 and now the relationship had run its course. Maybe there was a third party involved, it didn't matter if there was and all the more reason to call it a day.

We were married for only three years. The good intentions and feelings were there to start with. One could easily find blame in the age difference as Kirsty was much younger than me, or that I was away cruising now and again but she was well aware of these things when we met back in 1995. People change and for a relationship to work the foundations need to be rock solid from the start and there probably lies the reason. We moved on, it wasn't meant to be.

I left my wife for health reasons. I was sick of her!

Women are so changeable. When we first met, I adored her, now I can't stand her!

Just before the divorce I asked her, "One last time together for old time's sake?" She replied, "Over my dead body!" I said, "You haven't changed a bit!"

As we left the divorce court I said, "Goodbye mother of three." She replied, "Goodbye father of two!"

We have seen each other on the odd occasion over the years and all is fine between us, we have no regrets. Kirsty has met someone and has two children now and I wish her much happiness for the future.

Just before the break-up I had another setback. I had gone for a Well Health Assessment at a private clinic near my home. A health check costing a few bob but I felt it would be satisfying to get a clean bill of health now that I was not getting any younger!

Mind you, I felt as fit as a fiddle (why a fiddle –where did that come from?) I felt good, I'm not a big drinker and at the time was just a very casual smoker. I didn't like getting dressed up to have a ciggie!

I only smoked after a meal – I was on forty meals a day!

I tried to give up and went to see an Acupuncturist – he put pins in all my fags!

I went to see a Hypnotist and he put me under. Then he stole my cigarettes!

I said to the barman, "I've just put some money in the cigarette machine and it swore at me. The barman said, "That's out of order that!"

I asked my neighbour who was going on holiday if he could get me a carton of cigarettes. He came back and asked me for £75. I said, "That's a lot of money, where did you go?" He replied, "Bournemouth!"

I went to the gym now and again, played golf regularly and was exercising, however, I just needed confirmation that all was in good working order. I didn't want to overindulge in the long run, excuse the pun! I just wanted to see how fit I was I suppose.

I used to go to the pub five nights running!

I would skip breakfast, skip lunch – because skipping is good for you!

I even had a personal trainer: big bulging biceps, a six pack, strong hairy muscular legs – but she had lovely eyes!

I would do about six miles a day, then stop the car and run for ten minutes!

I would take three deep breaths every morning, open the window and climb in!

The health check cost £500, what a great way of losing a few pounds! It was very thorough and should have been for that money.

It ran over two days, excuse the pun again, and the overall conclusion was that I was in excellent health so I was well chuffed. But there were two problems.

Firstly, my cholesterol was sky high at 8.7! Straight away the doctor put me on statins, one every day for the rest of my life. He only gave me six… ha ha!

Today my cholesterol is around 5 which is ok. The second problem was blood in my stools again – no jokes about crap furniture thank you! I thought, here we go again, only this time I was advised to have a colonoscopy to check for cancer of the colon.

Another camera job and this time it was a bit more extensive. The endoscopy that I had previously had been like going through the Dartford tunnel, this time, however, they were going around the M25! The procedure was less embarrassing though thanks to sedation.

I remember saying to Simon the doctor, oh yes, we were on first name terms now, "How long will it take?" He replied, "We're finished!" Apparently, I did the same gag four times! I had a smile on my face and it was probably wind –and lots of it!

Once again, thankfully, the results were all clear. It was such a relief. I asked the doctor why there had been blood and his prognosis was that it was probably that stress would build up in the way of a cyst or fissure or similar and then burst every so often. It is always very essential to talk to your doctor and have these things checked out though.

On a brighter note my work was still flourishing and I had eight more cruises on Saga as the cast from Cocoon loved me!

I did two on the *Saga Pearl* which was a very small ship, the library doubled up as the show lounge but it gave the passengers somewhere to nap! The ship was first class throughout and the staff really looked after everybody so well.

The *Braemar, Aurora* and the *Thomson Spirit* were also full steam ahead. The beauty of cruising is that there is no driving up and down motorways at all hours of the day and night. After a show I can relax and have a drink and it is just a few yards walk or stagger back to my cabin at the end of the night!

I came out of the late bar a bit worse for drink and was walking along the corridor back to my cabin. The Captain was walking towards me and said, "You're staggering Mr Zany." I said, "You're not so bad yourself Captain!"

The Cabin Steward is hoovering the carpet on the ship and his boss said, "Can you hoover the carpet in the lift?" He said, "What, on every floor!"

A special cruise for me was on the *Saga Rose*, it was the Auckland to Sydney leg of a World cruise. I was still with Kirsty then just before she left for greener pastures, and she went on holiday to stay with her best friend who then lived in Christchurch, New Zealand, and I arranged to meet up with her in Sydney. Also, my two children Claire and James, were travelling for a year with their partners and after disembarking in Sydney they joined us for five days before we flew home.

I loved Sydney, the Opera House, the Bridge, sunbathing on Bondi Beach and we even took time out to go to the Comedy Store which was just outside the city.

Sailing into Sydney Harbour is an awesome experience and I do love the Aussies, they have a sense of humour to match the Brits.

I said to one, "Whereabouts are you from?" He replied, "I'm from the bush." I said, "I think you'll find we're all from the bush!"

In between cruises there was still the regular holiday centres and in addition the likes of Mill Rythe in Hayling Island, Seaton in Devon, Southdown in Chichester and Vauxhall in Great Yarmouth. With the economic recession looming changes would have to be made as more and more people began choosing holidays abroad where it was now as cheap as staying in the UK.

Also, the cruise ships were getting bigger and bigger and they were becoming more affordable to a wider range of people.

The Comedians Golfing Society held their annual Ball at the Grosvenor Hotel in Park Lane, London, and it was a great night and a chance to catch up with fellow comics.

On returning from Sydney we were invited to Reg's Fortieth Birthday Party (soz Shane's) in his back garden! This was a fab day, we stayed the night and saw lots of stars – we slept in an open topped tent! No, we stayed with Goz, of Wentworth fame and I can't believe that was over ten years ago now! Time is flying!

Another of my own Comedy nights was followed by a memorial for a lovely guy, an ex-Ipswich footballer called Dale Roberts who is sadly missed.

Private gigs and corporates were still popping up now and again, they made a refreshing change, but every now and then there would be a few one-offs which made life very interesting.

An Ipswich High School Sportsmen's Dinner with Jimmy Adams, the West Indies cricketer was followed by a riveting gig at the Age Concern Hall in Ware, Hertfordshire. Some comics would have hated that night working in a church hall full of OAP's still wearing their winter coats and scarves. Well it was July!

But not me and because of my new found fame with Saga, all went well. I had them eating out of my hand.....someone had forgotten the plates!

There are some lovely ladies here tonight....if only I was thirty years older!

He was so old he had an autographed Bible!

"How old are you Granddad?" "In dog years, I'm dead!"

People cross the road when they see my Granddad. He's a Lollypop man!

There was my own Christmas Cracker Comedy Show, then a Christmas party for a bunch of Suffolk Farmers and their farm hands (labourers). Nothing too clever was required here and they loved me having a go.

My mate went for a job on the local farm and asked, "Can you use me on the land?" The Farmer said, "No, we've got some special stuff for that!"

"Your boy has just broke my girl's virginity." "He's useless, he broke my tractor last week!"

"I've been putting manure on my rhubarb, what do you put on yours?" "Custard!"

One farmer to another, "How am I gonna get off this farmhouse roof?" The other replied, "Do like I did, jump in that load of manure, it's only ankle deep!" So he jumped off and landed up to his neck in the steaming hot manure. He shouted, "I thought you said it was only ankle deep?" He replied, "It was with me, I dived off head first!"

Chapter Thirty-Four

Don't Laugh At Me

2005 was here and before I was about to celebrate twenty five years as a pro, another special event happened which is one of the highlights of my career.

As a young lad I vividly remember the films of Norman Wisdom, Trouble in Store, A Stitch in Time, Bulldog Breed, Square Peg and many more. Norman was one of our funniest comedy actor performers ever and he was my hero and another legend.

I ended up working with the great man for two weeks on a Caribbean cruise –wow!

I shall always remember first meeting Norman, or should I say Sir Norman? He was leaning against the rail outside the restaurant on the Fred Olsen ship, *Braemar*. It is hard to describe how I felt. Here was my boyhood hero, comedy wise that is, and I was very nervous. The worst was yet to come, or it could have been the best, I'm not sure.

So I mumbled something like, "Hello Norman, I'm the comedian on the cruise, Micky Zany." It was hard to make out what he said which was not much really, he just mumbled and went into his familiar visual animation.

For some mad reason I began mimicking him. It was quite bizarre, there I was mucking around with the great Norman Wisdom. I couldn't believe it! I still get shivers thinking about it.....marvellous!

I was in my element over the next two weeks as you can imagine. He was such a humble man and every time we met I would do the walk, like a mirror image and the punters loved it!

Then came that special moment. On my first show I usually close my act with an impression of the great man himself. Every night of the cruise he would sit in the same place in the middle of the front row alongside his good friend and aide, Patrick, a lovely gentleman from the North East.

There I was about to do my impression, the first impression I did at that talent show with my cousin Steve back at Pontins, Pakefield, almost thirty years earlier.

What a feeling it was and such a surreal moment. Let this be the best Norman Wisdom impression I have ever done. He came backstage after the show and we had some photos taken and he mumbled in his own inimitable way, "You did me better than I do myself ". A very humble man and such a special moment for me.

Some moments are to be treasured forever and this was certainly one of them.

In May 2005 I celebrated twenty-five years as a professional and I took on the venture of hiring out the Regent, my local theatre, seating over one thousand five hundred people.

In hindsight it was a bit of a mistake, not because of the cost, but as it wasn't a great time for me personally and I wasn't in the right frame of mind.

My marriage break-up with Kirsty was a distraction and had become a bit messy. Firstly, she left wanting very little and then when push came to shove, other people got involved and then they want to squeeze you for every penny they can. I just wasn't prepared to put up a fight, it's not my way. Life's too short and you have to move on. I kept the house in the end with a slightly bigger mortgage!!

Nevertheless, the actual show went well and my great friend Peter Anthony compered with Karen Noble providing the singing, and a fantastic singer she is. The night was fun despite my mood and I have a DVD to remember it by.

Later that year, a pre-Christmas Caribbean cruise on *Braemar* was to be the first of many Caribbean Flagship Golf cruises right up until they stopped doing them in 2012.

My passion for golf made these particular cruises so much more appealing. Playing golf on the Caribbean islands with the golf pro and the passengers was fun and good PR work to boot! Ian Elzy Ellis and then Ian Harry Harrison were the golf Pros on these cruises and were two great characters! I do miss Harry's Bar!

As an extra gig I would perform a late show towards the end of the cruise which was always well received by the passengers who like their comedy with a little bit of sauce on the side!

I'll be using some four letter words that you are not used to hearing on a cruise ship ladies: Cook, dust, wash......!

In the alternative restaurant she asked, "Where do I get the omelettes from young man?" I replied, "Far queue. Far.....Queue!"

A posh lady said to the guy at Reception, "Do you have a complaints department?" He replied, "No we haven't you big, fat, spotty cow!"

An older gentleman celebrating his fifty years of marriage went to buy a see through nightie in the shop as a present for his wife. The assistant asks, "What size is she Sir?" He replied, "58....58.....58." She said, "What do you want to see through that for?!"

An elderly couple were sitting outside in the sunshine having their breakfast together. He asks, "Are you having a nice Golden Wedding celebration Hilda?" She replied, "Oh yes George, it's lovely on here, my breasts are all warm and tingly!" He said, "They should be, one's in your tea and the other's in your porridge!"

An old fella hobbled up to the ice- cream van and asked for a Knicker Bocker Glory. The ice-cream man asked, "Crushed nuts?" The old man said, "No, arthritis!"

Obviously, working with Norman was a major highlight for me but then low and behold, another hero of mine came along, not quite in the same domain as Mr Wisdom, but nevertheless gave me such a thrill.

It was April and I was asked to speak at the St. George's day registered charity at the Watford Hilton. What a wonderful lunch and afternoon, there was a jazz band, an opera singer, around six hundred men and a celebrity guest speaker, the one and only.....Sir Bobby Charlton!

Without sounding too melodramatic, here I was sitting next to another legend albeit in another field, a football one....ha ha!

Throughout lunch we chatted about football mainly. I told him my son was an avid Manchester United fan and I had taken him to the Theatre of Dreams on two occasions, both midweek European Cup matches.

He had no hesitation in offering us tickets anytime to go to Old Trafford – what a gentleman.

What was special about the St. George's Day lunch was that PC went out of the window. It was all about being English so obviously all others would be made fun of that was the order of the day, no matter where they came from. Yes, being

English was definitely top of the menu......Ding Dong!

The show went well and even the great man was laughing along with the large number in the audience. There seems to be an extra buzz which comes along with a corporate function of this size. My spot was very well received, so much so that I was asked back for the following two years. The guest speakers were Jimmy Greaves, another hero of mine and Will Greenwood, our World Cup winning rugby star. With the guest speakers being sporting heroes, gags on various sports would obviously be top of the list.

In Football, teams and managers who are not doing well:

The Manager has been done for speeding – well, its one way of getting three points!

An old fella was struggling with his shopping in the supermarket and a member of staff said, "Can you manage?" He replied, "I don't want the job!"

Glen Hoddle found God.....what a pass that was!

Ruud Guillet promised to play sexy football at Newcastle. He was right, they were getting f****d every week!

In cricket, England were struggling against the Indians. If you can't get the runs in India where can you get them!

I was watching Sumo wrestling for an hour and then realised I was watching darts!

On the telly was a dwarf basketball match. After nearly two hours it was still nil- nil!

I was at the races and a fella asked me, "Do you want the winner of the next race?" I replied, "No, I've only got a small garden!"

Do Boxers have sex before a fight? Only if they fancy each other!

I did eighteen cruises that year although some were quite short in length. The *Saga Ruby* was added to the *Rose*, with both these ships being much the same in size and the audiences were of comparable ages. When working on Saga I had to slow down somewhat and perform within myself and not be too Zany! To me it is basically about content and being clever, it is not what you do but more about what you don't do. It's not easy performing comedy, but then who wants easy.

A lady rang up the Doctor from her cabin and said, "I'm constipated." And they put her on hold!

Outside the medical centre an elderly lady was crying. I asked the Doctor, "Why is she crying so?" He said, "I told her she was pregnant." "Is she?" I asked. He said, "No, but it cured her hiccups!"

A man said, "Doctor, I've got these really bad headaches." The Doctor said, "I get them as well, do like I do. I rub my head along my wife's cleavage and this seems to do the trick, you want to try it." The next day the Doctor saw the man and asks, "Have they gone, the headaches?" He replied, "Yes, they've gone completely, and haven't you got a nice cabin!"

Every other week in the summer I was on the Thomson *Spirit*, nine cruises in all from Palma to Palma. These were so different in every department, compared to the more laid back atmosphere on Saga. To begin with the passengers didn't have to be over fifty and there were lots of families on Thomson so the choice of material had to be more suitable for the younger market. I was the only act on each cruise but my good mates Cruise Director, Stephen Guy and Assistant Cruise Director, Gavin Carroll, made me very welcome. We had a laugh.

I don't like spoilt kids. My six year old came home from school the other day not looking too happy. I asked, "What's the problem?" He said, "I'm so tired. The computer went down and we had to think!"

People say, "What will your boy be when he passes his exams?" I say, "28....29!"

He's just got his exam results and said to me, "Look dad, I've got a 'B' in reading." I said, "That's a 'D!'"

I now took a week off from performing to go on a golfing holiday with the lads from my Golf Club. It was Biarritz in France that year and I had to join them a day late because of work commitments but we had a fab week. There was lots of friendly banter and mickey taking and I wasn't expected to crack gags all the time. A week off was just what I needed and I wrote this poem about our golfing exploits and they loved it. Tommy, one of the lads, had it published in our local newspaper;

Biarritz 05

Micky got to the airport feeling rather glad,
Then Robbie rang, "We are all p****d, you'll have to get a cab!"
The cab had sat navigation, the driver asked me where,
He put in 'Victoria Surf', the voice said, "Don't go there!"

Lennie's won the money, you really have to hand it,
He may appear a musketeer, he's really quite a bandit!

Roger had lots of shots, he didn't want to lose,
His handicap next year is no fags or booze!

Phil has been the interpreter, his French is good it seems,
He has no problems with the menu, he's crap at reading greens!

Steve likes to have a laugh, he's been to see the quack,
Even though there are flaky bits, he still enjoys the crack,
He likes to have a drink and especially in France,
And when he goes to bed he piddles in his pants!

Geordie John, Y I Mon, each game he comes a cropper,
Every day he's had to pay, nice to not see a bent copper!

Keeny's golf's been up and down, he hasn't been a force,
His best drives all week, have been driving me and Tony to the course!

Eddies always horny, his sexual appetites not in a rut,
Poor old Colin's not the same, his sex life is just a putt!

This school is getting serious, they won't let me use the phone,
Graham shouted, "If that goes off, you'll be playing on your own!"

I don't know what all the fuss is about, it really is a farce,
At least I didn't use a napkin to wipe my frigging arse!

Mr Horsfield played quite well and at least he didn't sing,
A shout of fore is it Graham's ball, no it's his wedding ring!

Robbie's done a wonderful job, organizing us grumpy old men,
Forget the rooms and lack of girls, the golf's been 10 out of 10!

Who knows just where we will be next year, I'm sure it all depends,
We've hit the ball, said sod 'em all, let's drink to absent friends!

My playing partner Tony, who I used to room with, was the elder statesman of the party and he and the other lads used to come in for some stick now and again.

Tony said, "I can't get out of the bunker." I replied, "Keep your head down, take plenty of sand and follow through." He said, "I know that! It's ME that can't get out of the bunker!"

I said to my Scottish friend, "Why do you swing so fast?" He replied, "I had a ball pinched once!"

One of the lads was having a horrid time. He said, "I've never played this bad before." We all went, "You've played before?!"

He lost his ball in the ball washer!

He hit a birdie, an eagle, a rabbit and two chickens!

I said to him, "I know how you can take twelve shots off your handicap? Cut one of the holes out!"

He angrily replied, "If you keep making fun out of my golf, I'm gonna hit you with my four iron." To which I said, "you're a bit optimistic aren't ya?"

Trips to the south west and the south coast had almost stopped for me now. Travelling a long way to jobs would eventually take its toll on me, not that you had to pay a toll, well except the Dartford crossing!

On the other hand I kept the land gigs ticking over by relying on local venues. I was slowly updating and adding fresh material as this was always my mission. If I kept the holiday makers happy by changing my act they would keep coming back for more. Also, having lots of choices of material kept me fresh as well.

Vauxhall at Yarmouth, Potters at Hopton and Pakefield near Lowestoft were going strong and I still had my own shows and private functions as back up. However, it is obvious that cruising was and still is my mainstay and biggest earner.

Something a little different came along, a very small pub restaurant near Ipswich called The Capel White Horse. This venue was run by Roger Lee, formerly of Fred Olsen, and held about thirty-five people in all and turned out to be a fabulous night. It was very intimate, almost straight after the dinner and was like working in my lounge at home!

Compering is another format I enjoy – sometimes!

It gives me a chance to mix it with the boys and girls, localise, ad lib, get the crowd settled down, try out some new lines, be topical, but it is more important to not take the limelight away from the main acts or headliners. I like warming up an audience and find it quite satisfying and challenging.

On the Fred Olsen ships there is always a farewell show with all the acts and the show company. I get asked to compere these quite often which I enjoy doing at the end of a cruise.

I received my bar bill for the cruise and it was very high. I said to the lady at reception, "You've made a mistake with this bill?" She replied, "We have the chits" I said, "YOU'VE got the chits?!"

I had this girl banging on my door at 2am this morning. I had to get up and let her out!

225

Watch out at customs tomorrow. They're ok with booze and cigarettes but be careful with the biscuits and satchets of tea and coffee!

As you know I do enjoy a good gentlemen's evening, there is more license to go further. I did a sportsman's dinner at my local Legends Bar at Portman Road with many of the ex-Ipswich players attending. Then a few weeks later I was at our rivals bar, The Business Room at Carrow Road, Norwich. The content and approach would have to be somewhat different obviously. I liked to win both games! You could say I play for both sides – not in that way!

The Norwich evening wasn't ex-footballers, but a dinner for a haulage Company! They were hardened lorry drivers and they took no prisoners. They were a right bunch of truckers – I think that's what they described themselves as!

Down the years it is the travelling that becomes the downside to gigging. The jobs that are several hours away are now well and truly gone for me, well almost! Now that I am well established in the business I am able to work closer to home which is a far more comfortable feeling, keeping most of the travelling for cruise work.

Every now and then I get asked to go on Radio Suffolk with my very good friend Bob Shelley. Happy Hour on a Sunday morning is a guaranteed laugh and we put the world to rights in a very humorous way. Together with Foz, one of the DJ's from Radio Suffolk, I get the chance to mention any local shows coming up and soon I'll be on there to launch this book! Bob and I have done several shows together, he's a larger than life character and I wish him and his lady Lesley much love and happiness for the future.

Chapter Thirty-Five

Flying High

Constantly working on the act over many years now was certainly paying off in terms of adding fresh ideas and observational humour to the ever growing routines. It definitely pays having routines about all and sundry especially on ships. You'd be surprised at what people say, the daft things you hear on board a ship!

The wife says, "He was funny wasn't he George?" He replied, "Yes, if you like laughing!"

The husband says, "You must be funny mate, the wife only slept through half of it!"

'Why aren't you on the telly with all that other crap?!'

On a trip to Egypt once, "Why did they build the Pyramids so far from the port?!"

Visiting Pompeii one time, "Why did the Romans build so many ruins?!"

When we were docked in Rome one day a passenger was heard to say to a friend, "I'll meet you in the Vatican." To which his mate asked, "Bar or Lounge?!"

There was more cruising on *Oriana*, *Oceana*, *Arcadia* and *Aurora* for P&O, then *Braemar*, *Black Prince* and *Boudicca* for Fred Olsen and I was rubbing shoulders again with some very talented acts.

I have never been away at Christmas and this last trip on *Boudicca* was the first time I had spent New Year's Eve at sea. I was single again and it was nice to socialise and celebrate the New Year with others including my good friend, Linzi Milne, the Hotel Manager on the *Braemar*. We saw the New Year in with a drink or two!

A night at the Bescot Stadium, Walsall, with Joe Brown and his Bruvvers was special. He hadn't changed a bit and was still doing the business after all these years.

Another superb night was had at a golf club in Morpeth, near Leeds with Patti Gold and Stuart Atkins. I then had a welcome return to the Broadstairs Pavilion with my old mucker Rob Rawles which rounded things off nicely.

A second Golf Charity Day at my Golf Club in Rushmere was another success raising money once again for the children at the St. Elizabeth Hospice. I also added my leisure club at Martlesham to the list of gigs. There was around one hundred people in the bar area, another intimate evening which was well received by the members.

My gym instructor said, "We need to put two inches on your chest." I replied, "Right measurement, wrong place!"

Where's your six pack? I've drunk them all!

I don't do weights –they're bloody heavy!

They have a new machine at our gym, it does everything: Mars bars, Kit Kats, Crisps......!

It is mostly regulars that come to these comedy shows and I felt that it was getting harder to promote and sell the tickets, so I thought it was right to take time out and that a break was needed. Remember, familiarity breeds contempt! Sometimes, less is more!

I met a brilliant Elvis impersonator, Miguel, and we worked together several times for a mutual friend called Vic Dennis, whose Christmas office parties were phenomenal, great events. There were many acts there including Salsa bands, you name it, he had it!

It was from these extravaganzas that Miguel asked me to work with him at yet another Chinese restaurant, The Lotus House in Canary Wharf which was a floating restaurant!

Three times I went there and it was certainly different from the norm. There was a running buffet.......how to eat and keep fit at the same time!

I had a Chinese last night – nice girl!

I went out with a Chinese girl. She was really sweet.....and sour!

Whenever you order a take away on the phone they always say five to ten minutes, no matter how big the order is!

I said, "Do you deliver?" He replied, "No, just chicken and beef!"

A robber went in and said, "Give me all the money out of the till?" The assistant asks, "To take away?"

Then Elvis came on with his backing singers and dancers. What a night, Viva Las Vegas – Chinese style!

Restaurant gigs seemed to be all the fashion at that time and I returned to the White Horse pub just outside Ipswich to a capacity crowd of thirty-four, another sell out!

The Hunters Meet restaurant at Hatfield Heath with Brendan was a great place to work and very intimate as well. Then I did Bentleys restaurant in Ipswich with my great buddy Leo Shavers and the late Joe Goodman....who was the king of the one-liners and a very funny man. God bless him.

The corporate golf days were indeed becoming a speciality.   One such gig was with a very dear friend Johnny Clark, who used to compere at the notorious Kings Club at Canvey Island back in the eighties. Johnny was looking after the corporate hospitality now at Langdon Hills Golf Club near Basildon and he gave me quite a few after dinner golf days and so forth culminating in a very funny night at Chelmsford Cricket Club with Phil Tuffnell, now of A Question of Sport fame.

With the economic recession fast approaching, some of the corporate work diminished as did some of the regular haunts that had been going for years. Unfortunately, the nights at the major holiday centres and also the smaller private ones slowly got less and less.

All good things come to an end. Some of the venues lowered their budgets and then travelling long distances to these gigs would no longer be viable for me.

Fred Olsen's newly acquired *Boudicca* the sister ship to the *Black Watch* was going well, followed by *Aurora* and then back to back cruises on the *Braemar* again. The *Saga Ruby* came in once more and this would be my last Saga cruise for four years from Sydney to Honolulu. I'm sure that to the average man in the street cruising sounds so glamourous and as long as I did well on stage it was a great atmosphere but filling in the spare time in a positive way was also important to me.

The travelling to and from the ships can be very harrowing and stressful and flying around the world has its moments!

I flew first class with Ryan Air! I flew from Norwich International Airport!

Norwich International Airport is the only airport in the world where the runway has a cattle grid on it.

Ryan Air........used to be called Air-fix!

I rang them up, "How much to Tenerife?" The man said, "Do you want the price or the odds?"

I got an upgrade, they gave me a seat!

When you put the reading light on, the plane slowed down a bit!

We flew beside a British Airways plane for two hours to watch their film!

Flying back from Honolulu to Heathrow via Chicago and Washington is quite a journey if all goes well and to time. Unfortunately, when you take off one hour late from the first airport you know that it's going to be touch and go, in this case it was touch and stop!

I missed the first connecting flight at O'Hare Airport and was asked to wait twenty-four hours for the next corresponding flight which was a bit of a pain to say the least!

As luck would have it there was a 5.00 pm flight that evening direct to London

Heathrow and I asked to go on the standby list. Low and behold I managed to get the last seat at the very last minute. I had no idea where my luggage was and I eventually got it back a week later!

I'd rather sail than fly any day. If something happens to the ship I can at least swim a bit. If something happens to a plane I can't fly an inch!

Then followed a three day cruise to Amsterdam and back which was a walk in the park after the last eleven weeks!

I like Holland, I speak a little Hollish!

I like window shopping! I have always wanted to be a window cleaner in Amsterdam!

I went out with a Dutch girl, she wore those inflatable shoes. We didn't last long, she popped her clogs!

Me and Tristian, the sound engineer from the ship, were loitering around the streets of Amsterdam like a couple of naive adolescents, daring each other to go into one of the places that sold broth, to sample the goods! Common sense did prevail and our self-pride got the better of us, not that we would have actually sampled anything of course!

This woman came up to me and said, "You can sleep with me for fifty Euros. I replied, "I'm not very tired but the money will come in handy!"

One lady of the night said to the other, "I must have been up these stairs a hundred times today." The other replied, "oh, your poor feet!"

After a further three cruises on *Arcadia*, two on the *Black Watch* and then the *Braemar* and the *Boudicca* I was more than glad to be cruise free from October onwards in more ways than one.

On the 25th October 2007 my dear mum went into hospital. She was in there a week and never came out.

It was the worst moment of my life.

Chapter Thirty-Six

Save Me a Front Seat Mum

My mum left us too soon and although she was in her eightieth year she still had so much life left to live. She had never been ill or in hospital before so it came as such a shock when she was admitted with what seemed to be a minor problem. My mum, Barbara Daphne, always had something to talk about, she would light up any room when she walked in. A very astute woman, my mum could talk to you about any subject from world affairs to sporting issues or personal problems at home.

Whatever good qualities, inner strength and mental toughness I have is all down to my dear mum.

It was 11.07 am on Friday the 2nd November that she took her last breath and left this life. Heaven is now a much better place and I can hear her now telling the good people up there all about her family and how proud she is of her funny boy!

I only wish she was here today to see how happy I am now and to meet Lesley, the love of my life. She didn't like me being on my own, I could tell that, and I would often joke with her that I would end up with a hot blooded foreign girl, and I have, Lesley is from the northern hemisphere – Manchester!

I also feel sad that my mum did not get to see her great granddaughter, Matilda Daisy, and her great grandson, Toby James.

To think in November 2007 I lost my mum and two weeks after the funeral I gave my daughter away as she got married. It was a very happy occasion but obviously sad at the same time in that Claire's grandma could not be there to share the joy. My Claire looked stunning in her fabulous dress.

One year later my first grandchild was born – highs and lows life is full of them!

It's funny you know, when something or someone special is taken away from you and you then realise just how much they meant to you. I still find it difficult to think that my mum is no longer here, in body that is. She is always in my mind. She was so proud of what I had achieved so far in this crazy show business world! It was Thursday the 25th October and I was suited and booted and ready to go to a corporate function, a golf dinner in Essex. It was around 5.00 pm and my mobile rang and it was my sister Jan. She was frantic, she always sounds frantic! She said she was taking mum to the hospital as she had tummy pains and severe constipation. That didn't sound too bad to me – constipation, and I made my way to the hospital to meet them.

By the time I arrived at the hospital Jan was in a panic, more so than usual and she told me that they were taking mum to intensive care. Intensive care for constipation, I didn't understand? I was speaking to mum at her bedside and we chatted quite lightheartedly as I was trying to keep her spirits up. She didn't really say too much and I remember her just staring at me. I believe now in hindsight that she knew that something was seriously wrong. The doctor called us into a side room and said, "It's not good, we're not quite sure but…" the words were coming out of his mouth but my mind was miles away and the words were not sinking in.

I was starting to get negative thoughts, my mum in a serious condition, don't be stupid, she was fine earlier it's just constipation. She will live forever.

I simply could not imagine life without my dear mum. I went back to see her and did not want to seem too anxious or to let her think that anything was seriously wrong. How stupid was I? My mum knew, she knew everything.

Anyway, within minutes she was all piped up and for the next week she was away with the fairies. She was tired and all worn out. All those years of looking after everybody else, especially my dad, and always worrying and being concerned for her family had taken its toll.

We were told that she had pancreatitis and that not many people recover from that especially at her age. One week later she was gone. My greatest love had been taken away. They say that time is a great healer but it still hurts even today.

Mum had known that I wasn't happy, I made out that I was ok but she knew. I kept those feelings to myself. She wanted me to be with someone, someone who could love me like she did, take care of me and be as proud of me as she was Well, if you can hear me now mum, I think I have, I'm sure I have found that someone…..LOL!

At the end of the day, my sister and I were both glad that on that fateful Friday morning when she took her last breath she didn't suffer and we are so grateful for that.

Since mum has passed on, Jan and I have become much closer. Jan is strong just like mum and cared for our dad until his passing three years later in January 2011.

I certainly could not have done what she did. Bless you Jan.

I didn't work for a while after mum died and I took time out. I wasn't at all in the mood to be funny.

While my mum was in hospital I had been booked to do a corporate function for Fred Olsen at the Belfry in Sutton Coldfield. It was a sales conference for travel agents and so forth. Not wanting to let them down I drove up and then straight back again after the gig. It went well and I can't think why because my mind was miles away – literally, it was a long drive back.

In a strange way I think I have become a much stronger person since my mum went. Her passing has given me a greater determination and an extra purpose in life with an ambition to go further.

Life is short – grab every moment.

I only wish that I had been with someone at that time. Someone to hold and someone to hold me. I felt more alone than ever before.

Claire, James and my sister Jan were there and that was important.

The funeral was difficult, obviously. Just as it would be for anyone. The church was packed as everyone loved my mum. I did the eulogy and I just about held it together.....just.

Afterwards we had a wake at which as well as mourning mum's passing we celebrated her life. I wanted to be just a little bit lighthearted in the church just to break the ice a little. She would have liked that and this is what I said;

I was on a Saga ship and because of the satellite delay on the phone, to stop us talking over each other, I asked mum to say 'over' when she had finished talking. Well she tried bless her and then kept forgetting, so would say it five or ten seconds later over me speaking! We laughed on the phone, it was like a comedy sketch. Looking up at the church ceiling I said, "Do you remember that mum? Over!" I still laugh and cry at that even today.

Going to the Chapel of Rest to see my mum a couple of days after she died with Jan was very difficult and is not a moment that I want to remember too much, it wasn't my mum anymore.

However, they say life goes on as we all know and the day my daughter Claire got married was a truly wonderful occasion. My little girl looked absolutely stunning.

The father of the bride speech was not easy for me and I had to stop halfway to hold back the tears. Claire came over and gave me a hug, we consoled each other and remembered together our wonderful mum and grandma.

It was strange that I had no cruises planned for October, November and the December of that year. Things happen for a reason and I believe that even more so now.

That was a tough Christmas for me on my own. My daughter was on her honeymoon in Tanzania, James was away in Sweden with his Swedish girlfriend and my mum was spending Christmas with the angels.

I have never been away at Christmas as it is a time for family. This was one Christmas I was happy to forget.

Chapter Thirty-Seven

Midnight Madness

A new year and new beginnings, well almost.

It was back to the Caribbean on the *Braemar* for me with three cruises in a row for six weeks. I felt like I needed it and it was just the tonic.....with a few gins added as well!

Cruising over the years, as I have said, has opened up many opportunities for different comedy subject matter. The most common denominator is probably telling jokes and doing lines from the places that the passengers came from. Whether it be a short around Britain cruise to a worldie, there is always a wide range of language and accent material. It certainly makes contact and breaks down a lot of barriers.

I was now regularly doing a late night comedy spot for those that like their material a bit more edgy and racier with just a hint of innuendo. If they were going to be offended by some spicier or off the wall type humour then they wouldn't be expected to attend the 11.30 pm session!

I rang the doctor, "I've got this premature e-jack, e-jack, e......
I'll have to call you back!"

The doctor rang back, "How is it?" I said: "Touch and go!"

A lady complained to the doctor of itching sensation up her bum. When she bends over there is a piece of lettuce sticking out! "Is it serious?" she asks the doctor. He replied, "It's just the tip of the iceberg!"

A fella goes into hospital for a vasectomy. After the operation, the surgeon is beside himself and very distraught. "I'm very very sorry but we've given you a sex change by mistake!" The man can't believe it and asks, "Will I still be able to get an erection?" The Surgeon replied, "You will, but it won't be yours!"

In Morocco I bought a genuine leather purse from a market stall. The man said the leather was from the skin of a donkey's manhood! When you stroke the purse, it turns into a suitcase!

It had now been almost twenty years that I had worked with P&O and ten years with Fred Olsen and it was always a pleasure to work for both companies. After the *Braemar* Caribbean cruises, came the *Boudicca* and *Black Watch* and then *Aurora* and *Arcadia* again, working with my mates, singers Jamie Michael Stewart, Jane Beaumont, Robbie Allen, the multi- talented Caroline Dennis and the very funny, larger than life, comedy magician Jimmy Carlo. In between these I continued to do the tried and tested, the bread and butter regular gigs as I like to call them.

There are many instances and situations which happen and will never be repeated but will stick in my memory forever.

On a theatre show one night on *Aurora*, a well-dressed couple came into the theatre a few minutes late. It was a formal night and the stunning lady sauntered elegantly down the side of the theatre in her ball gown with her husband a few steps behind. She looked a million dollars like Sophia Loren and Gina Lollobrigida rolled into one, so very glamourous and beautiful.

I came off the stage, took her hand, and as I was escorting her to an empty seat I asked her where she was from. She remarked in a very broad, loud, Essex accent, SARFEND! (Southend). The audience burst into hysterical laughter, the mood changed and I let her find her own seat! The reason I mention this is that every time I meet my good friend the Cruise Director Neil Oliver, who was on *Aurora* at the time he always comes out with, SARFEND?! You had to be there.

A small restaurant in Ipswich called The Brasserie booked me for a few comedy nights, add in some golf dinners and the first half of the year was certainly a busy one. There was no time to even see a relationship on the horizon.

There was no one at home except my son James and I loved him being there with me, not only as a son but as my best mate as well and we spent some quality time together.

A new adventure turned up for me in the shape of Royal Caribbean Cruise Lines (RCCL) sailing on the *Independence of the Seas*. I have not yet mentioned that Royal Caribbean came calling a year ago. It wasn't the dream start I had hoped for and in fact, it was a bloody nightmare.

To begin with my good friend and booker for the American Lines, Jo Martin, told me I would be embarking the RCCL *Navigator of the Seas* in Southampton. At the eleventh hour that was changed to the *Jewel of the Seas* embarking in Harwich not too far from where I lived.

The RCCL ships are massive. The *Oasis of the Seas* weighs in at 220,000 tonnes compared to the baby *Braemar* which is only 23,000 tonnes. Once again girls, size is not important, is it?!

When I arrived at Harwich I was greeted with, "I'm afraid that you're not on the manifest and the Cruise Director does not have a slot for you to perform." Charming, nice to feel wanted then!

I was then about to phone my son to get him to come and pick me up when someone came back and said all had been changed and I was now going on the ship.

It was a long three days and I was told that I'd be doing a late show on the third night of the cruise, which was the night before Tallinn, in Estonia, when I would be disembarking. It was a midnight show, with no band, no rehearsal, nothing! What a great introduction to a cruise company for me.

The only good fortune was that one of my favourite acts Joe Longthorne was on and I had someone to have a drink or two with. Joe was also performing that third night at 7.00 pm and 9.00 pm and I had to wait until nearly midnight before my show in the one thousand, seven hundred seater theatre.

For some bizarre reason I thought that I had nothing to lose and that I had been put in a corner so I just went for it!

Once again experience counts for everything. There was a minority of English passengers but it was predominantly Americans that made up the audience and younger ones at that!

On the end of the front row was the Cruise Director who as yet had not even spoken to me!

Anyway, throwing caution to the wind as they say, I had a really satisfying thirty minutes. It felt more like a comedy store environment with the younger age group and the late hour.

Straight after the show the Cruise Director was very complimentary to me and consequently I have sailed with RCCL many times since.

What a fickle business this is. Still, as you've probably gathered by now, I do love a challenge!

So now I'm on the *Independence of the Seas* with another one thousand, seven hundred seat theatre and an orchestra to die for. I did two more cruises on that ship in August and October. It is more like a floating hotel with three and a half thousand passengers. These ships provide a fantastic holiday for all the family with everything available, including a concrete abseiling wall and a Flow-rider which is a surfing pool at the back of the ship.

The alternative buffet restaurant at the top of the ship, the Windjammer, is enormous and bigger than the *Braemar* ship itself! There was food everywhere, twenty-five hours a day, eight days a week!

They have an abseiling wall on the big American ships. Can you imagine a climbing wall on this little ship? Who's gonna climb that? Unless there was a buffet on top!

Mind you, the Americans do like their food. One lady in the self service restaurant had so much on her plate. She said, "I've got an overactive thyroid." I said, "I think you've got an over active knife and fork!"

She then said, "I think my eyes are bigger than my belly." I replied, "No, no, no, no no....no!"

Then she said, "I've got problems with my feet." I said, "You have, they won't leave the restaurant!"

Still they do say, the more you eat the cheaper the cruise!....and some of you will end up saving a fortune!

There were more trips on *Aurora*, *Oriana* and *Oceana* and now the new Olsen acquisition, the *Balmoral*. Not quite the size of the Independence, but a lot more intimate and friendly with a great cabaret lounge.

I had some friends on this cruise with me from the golf club, there were six couples in all, including my close friends John and Andrea McNally. It was extra special having them on.

It's also a pleasure to work with the new Cruise Directors on Fred Olsen, Anthony 'Boz' Borrodale, Ricky Jermy, Simon Vickers and Jackie Probert.

I was in the public toilet on the ship, sitting in trap 1 and there must have been someone else in trap 2. A voice said, "How are ya?" I hesitantly replied, "I'm fine thank you." He then said, "Weather's not too bad?" I said, "Yeah it's ok." He then asked, "How are the kids?" I replied, "They're ok, I think." All of a sudden, a head came over the top of the cubicle wall and he said, "Do you mind mate, I'm on my mobile phone!"

If all this wasn't enough what with Olsen, P&O, Saga and RCCL then along came the prestigious Cunard line.

The *Queen Mary II* is slightly more upmarket and there were no casual nights and a lot of Americans to boot. I worked with a great Welsh singer called Eve Sharratt on that cruise. The Royal Court Theatre is a wonderful venue and very salubrious.

Coincidentally, it was the first anniversary of my dear mum's passing and I can remember thinking how proud she would have been if she could see me now performing on this very classy cruise liner. It was awfully posh and I loved it, though I had to adapt somewhat! It seems the more you pay, the less you laugh. I'd hate to be rich!

After this cruise I did a one-off theatre show at the Westcliff in Clacton-on-Sea with my old mate Jimmy Jones. It was good to see and work with him once again.

My own comedy show, A Christmas Cracker, was a nice way to end the year......well almost.

Along came a moment of madness. I was about to get wed for the third time!

I know what you're thinking ....!

2003 me in Rio
(no, it's not the Angel of the North)

2003 (Black Watch)
St. Peters Square in Rome -
waiting for the Pope!

2003 (Black Watch)
Colliseum, Rome

March 2002 on Aurora with
the classy Bonnie Langford

2002 on Black Watch
with Sid Little

2002 Summer Show on
Black Watch with Andrew
Robley, Stevie Hewlett,
(Tiny Tina) and John Bell

Black Watch in 2002
with Stevie and John

242

2003, 1st Saga Rose Cruise with
Cruise Director Roy Parkinson

Saga Rose 2003
sailing into Sydney Harbour

September 2004
on Saga Pearl with
Edwina Currie and
husband John

Saga Rose 2004 with
Elaine Delmar

P&O Oceana 2003
with Gary & Paul

Thomson Spirit 2004 with
Cruise Director Stevie Guy

Me with James & Shane
outside Eastenders Studio
2004

Thomson Spirit 2004
with my son James

2005 on Braemar with
my hero, the 'legend'
Sir Norman Wisdom

2004 at Potters, Hopton with David Essex

Black Watch with Scott Paige

Braemar '05 with Dave 'the Russian'

Braemar May '06 with my buddy Leo Shavers

246

On Saga in Greenland - there's nothing there!

The Spanish golfing holiday with my partner and buddy Tony 'Godfather' Adams, 2011

Fred Olsen 'Braemar' with Nick, Leo, Willy and Ian 'Elzy' Ellis

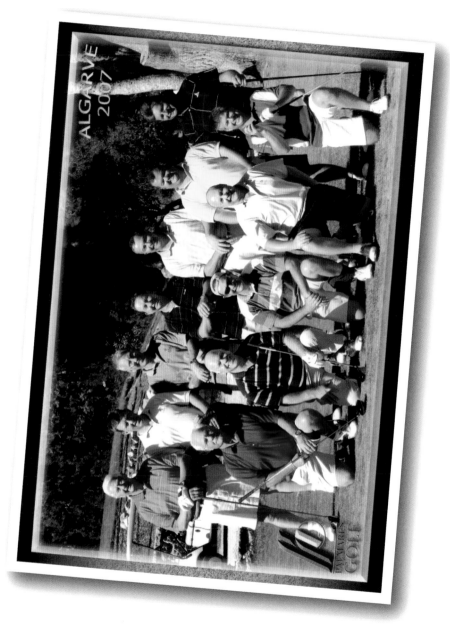

The jolly boys golf outting

World curise on Aurora Jan '07 with Caroline Dennis, Maria King, Dick Van Wynkle and Robbie Allen

Boudicca 2007 with Melody Lane

Black Watch 2007 with Allan Stewart and Sonia (Melody Lane)

Arcadia 2007
with Hilary O'Neil

2007 on Saga Rose world
cruise with Esther Rantzen

Arcadia 2007
with
Bobby Crush

Me and my Dear Mum

2008 on Queen Mary II
with Eve Sharratt

2008 backstage at the
Regent Theatre, Ipswich
with Joe Pasquale

2009 on Grand Princess
with Stevie The Vent!

Boudicca 2010 with Jim
Bowen and wife Phyliss

252

2011 on Braemar
with Leo and Harry
the Golf Pro

P&O Azura 2011
with Martin Daniels
and George King

Anna and Eamon,
our Matchmakers!

2011 A night out with Claire and James,
just before he flew out to Hanoi, Vietnam

Myself and Lesley gigging with the very funny
Jimmy Cricket - come 'ere, and there's more!

'Braemar' with Ian, Linzi, Jamie, myself and Lesley with Sue on her birthday!

My first hole in One - March 2004 (I managed to do it again in 2014)

The Village Idiot

Chapter Thirty-Eight

Third Time Unlucky

Hindsight is a wonderful thing.

It is fair to say that I was at a low ebb, in my personal life that is, and quite a bit vulnerable, which might sound like a half-hearted excuse. I was lost!

I was always hoping to find that someone really special to spend the rest of my life with.

There must be many professions that make life a little bit testing now and again and I suppose being married to an entertainer who has to be away at times would have its moments. Surely any relationship in any walk of life has to be worked at and small sacrifices have to be made on both sides?

Anyway, significant other number three came along and what seemed like a good idea and promising to start with, never took off. I was wrong. We had made a mistake. Simple as that. It was all over in under a year and I still can't understand why it happened. I'm stunned that I went through with the wedding so quickly and to be honest I did try to call it off a few weeks before. I was stupid when I think about it, mind you, I don't think about it too often, trust me!

Hence 2009 had its trials and tribulations! Work-wise, I did another three Caribbean golf cruises for Fred Olsen, two on *Oriana*, the *Independence* and a debut on the *Grand Princess*, Naples to Gibralter, with my buddy Steve Hewlett.

There are some great ports where I could use stock material. In Naples, for instance, crossing the road from the port to the city centre is a nightmare as you can imagine especially how the Italian's drive!

Crossing the road here is another one of nature's best laxatives!

In England we drive on the left, in Europe on the right, in Naples...optional!

Gibraltar is well known for tax free items and most passengers take advantage of buying cheap goods there.

There has been so much booze brought back onto the ship, we had to leave twenty passengers behind!

We're funny us Brits. We pay a thousand pounds for a cruise to save twenty pounds on drink!

It's nice to see a bottle of Mateus Rose without a candle in it!

Along came a debut on P&O's new *Ventura*, a ship much in the same style as the *Grand Princess*, weighing in at around 115,000 Tonnes. Unbeknown to me the next time I worked on *Ventura* would turn out to be a life changing experience!

This was to be another successful year of cruising with a chance to impress again on Cunard on their new liner the *Queen Victoria*. The theatre was to die for and the material, like on Saga had to be carefully chosen.

The 'Kentucky Fried Pheasant' and the 'Bags under the eyes Gucci' gags were perfect for this clientele.

I asked for a bottle of water. She came back and asked, "Still water?" I said, "Yes, I haven't changed my mind!"

Do you like the suit? I got it from Armani. Armani and Navy!

A lady was in the Library, "Do you have any plays by Shakespeare?" The girl replied, "Which one?"And the lady said, "William!"

How to speak posh, pronounce the words AIR, now HAIR, and then LAIR. Now say them together.....Air Hair Lair!

With another seventeen weeks at sea, a few one-offs and the regular haunts I'd had another year to look back on with great satisfaction. I always found it so rewarding to go back to the tried and tested venues and I went there with a certain amount of confidence but also never took anything for granted.

I was still adding new material keeping the act fresh and always thinking on my feet. Talking of new material, along came a new addition to the family, a gorgeous granddaughter!

My first grandchild, Matilda Daisy, was born on the 29th December 2008 at 9.33 pm weighing in at 6lb 12oz.

Why do people tell men the weight of a baby? Do we really want to know? We don't say, here's the wife, fourteen stone ten!

I was in shock when Claire rang me. No warning, no build up, no going into labour, waters broke – nothing! She said, "Dad, your granddaughter is ten minutes old and she's beautiful!" I could not believe my little girl had had a baby, what an indescribable feeling.

A month later my marriage to number three had more or less broken down. It had gone from bad to worse and even to the point that I was glad to go away cruising on my own and I haven't said that very often!

There was very little communication towards the end and there was no way back. As a well-known film character once said.......... 'Life is like a box of chocolates.......you never know what you're gonna get! Stupid is what stupid does.....that's all I got to say about that!'

"I'm gonna make you the happiest guy in the world." "I'll miss ya!"

They start off as Snow White or Cinderella, then finally turn into the Wicked Witch, Anne Robinson, "You are the weakest link.....goodbye!"

She said she needed space – so I locked her outside the house!

I said, "You're leaving me because I'm impotent." She said, "No hard feelings!"

She said I didn't pay her enough attention. I think that's what she said, I wasn't really listening!

She said we didn't communicate, so I sent her an email saying..... 'We do!'

We just weren't compatible. I'm a Sagittarius and she was a pain in the arse!

We shared a sense of humour, we had to, she didn't have one!

As it was all coming to an end I was invited to do the inaugural cruise on the brand new P&O *Azura* the twin sister ship to the *Ventura.*

It was when the dust cloud had filled the air from the volcano in Iceland and air space was shut down. Instead of joining halfway into the cruise we had to

259

wait several days and finally join in Gibraltar! It became a three dayer back to Southampton but it was very flattering and satisfying to be asked to do it.

I came back to an empty house, it was such a relief and I was a very happy bunny.

My mate and great comedian John Martin, from Liverpool, funny guy Martin Daniels, Russell Watson and his orchestra and myself were all due to fly out to pick up the *Azura* in Croatia. Delays due to the ash cloud no fly zones meant that we couldn't fly out when we were supposed to.

A funny situation occurred – well it was for me at the time – on the Thursday before we actually flew out to Gibraltar on the Sunday.

My agent Barry and I had been sent an email late on the Wednesday evening saying that I was due to fly out to Korkula, Croatia, at 6.30 am the following morning.

Neither of us were at home or online so we knew nothing of this re-arranged flight time.

The following morning I was playing golf at my home club and was coming down the ninth fairway and received a call on my mobile phone. It was the agent in Croatia who said, "You are not at the airport Mr. Lander?" I said, "No, I'm on the ninth fairway at my golf club!" She replied, "Is Donald Sinden with you?" Obviously, he must have been booked to do a lecture or talk on the cruise as well – remember Donald Sinden, the actor, TV's Never the Twain with Windsor Davies? I flippantly replied, "No he's not, but he may be on the back nine!" You had to be there!

A Croatian shipping agent ringing me on my mobile on my golf course in Ipswich, how times have changed!

Cruising jokes have stood the test of time as does a lot of other material. Most jokes, when they are past their sell by date, can be re-vamped or updated.

Somebody asked if it was sea water or fresh water in the swimming pool? A man replied, "It must be sea water, it's always bloody rough!"

When they do the ice carving they always say weather permitting. Surely you want cold weather?!

They said they were going to turn a block of ice into a work of art. A bit like my ex-wife but the other way round!

Chapter Thirty-Nine

Losing Dad

Another chapter, or should I say marriage, was over.

It just happened to coincide with my thirtieth anniversary in the business as a pro. There was no celebration this time just a quiet one I enjoyed on my own. It was also a sad time. My father could no longer cope at home even with Jan and four carers going in daily and he inevitably had to go into care. His health was slowly deteriorating both physically and mentally with the onset of dementia.

Once my mum had gone it was the start of the end for dad. To some extent my mum had been his carer for many years.

His first care home wasn't up to much but he later moved into a second home run by Bupa and it was so much better. It happened to be on the Maidenhall Estate in Ipswich which is coincidentally where I was born. Not in the care home I hasten to add!

It was so sad to see him there, those that have, or have had loved ones in care will understand. Don't get me wrong the staff were brilliant and my dad seemed to be at ease and was friendly towards them. However, his dementia seemed to be getting worse as the days went by. Strange as it may sound I felt I had to find humour at this time to cope with the frustration and fragility of the situation.

I was asked to do a gig at a care home. It was at St. Peter's Close in Gravesend.... a bit ironic I thought!

An old fella said to a lady at the dinner dance, "Do I come here often?"

She said, "Act your age."... and he died!

She said, "Take me up stairs and make passionate love to me." He said, "I can't do both!"

Three old fellas talking. One said, "I have ten cigars in the morning, ten cigars in the afternoon and ten cigars at night and next month I'll be eighty six." The second old fella says, "I have ten beers in the morning, ten beers in the afternoon and ten beers at night and next week I'll be seventy four. The third one says, "I have ten women in the morning, ten women in the afternoon and ten women at night and on Monday I'll be twenty two!"

My dad and I never had the same loving relationship that I had with my mum. It would frustrate me no end that he showed little ambition and adventure in his later years.

He had retired in his early fifties and almost gave up. There is living and there is living life. Mind you, he never lost his sense of humour. He may have lost his memory somewhat and had dementia but whenever I cracked a funny there would invariably be a smile on his face. He seemed a million miles away in that care home but I would look around and try to lighten the situation. It wasn't easy sometimes!

A refreshing change came along when I was asked to host a local awards dinner for Argent, which was part of the local Evening Standard newspaper. It was a recruitment awards evening at the Belstead Brook Hotel in Ipswich and it was good to be doing another corporate gig. I announced the winners of the various categories so there was plenty of scope to do some funnies in between each one. Although you can be a bit too clever sometimes, it was mainly a younger audience and some of them were eager to get juiced up or leathered as they tend to say, at the thought of a free bar!

The first award I did with my back to the audience looking behind me and after a few lines, I turned around;

I haven't always been a comedian – I used to be a taxi driver! (Subtle, I know, but a good time to do it!)

I used to work in the Post Office. It didn't last long as they would play music in the background and every time the music stopped I would undo a parcel!

I used to work in a library – I kept that quiet!

A fella went into the DIY section and asked the librarian: "Do you have any books on shelves?"

I went for a job as a window cleaner – I had to do a smear test!

I worked in a nursery growing Bonsai Trees. We were that successful we had to move to smaller premises!

This gig was followed a few weeks later by another property awards dinner, again it was a black tie event with another free bar. This time a thirty minute stand up was asked for having fun with, once again, a much younger audience. This is often a refreshing change from the age of the passengers on the cruise ships.

There followed one more event in this trilogy for the East Anglian Daily Times. It was the Best Bar None Awards and inside knowledge of the local inns and pubs would help me to get the audience warmed up. I like hosting and compering and involving the audience and their establishments in the act certainly helps me no end.

My annual golfing holiday with the lads followed a cruise on *Arcadia*, then a dozen gigs or so, a pre-Christmas Caribbean cruise on *Braemar* and a New Year's Eve show at my own golf club brought another successful year to a close.

No sooner had we seen the New Year in when the inevitable happened.........
Dad was gone.

Chapter Forty

When North Meets South

People have asked were you there when Claire and James were born and I reply that I was, and that it was a great feeling and a wonderful experience. Nothing compares to it.

Another significant life experience was seeing my mum and dad take their last breath which is very traumatic. It felt better knowing that my sister and I were there for mum and dad. Surely we would all want our loved ones by our side at the end and it seemed to bring closure in a very spiritual way as well. This will depend on the individual relationship obviously, more so for me with my mum as we could not have been closer.

With my dad it was a different scenario completely as he had suffered for long enough and it was a relief. It was his time to go.

With both my parents now passed on and me single again, it was important for me to maintain the passion and drive for my work. Feeling sorry for myself and just going through the motions was not an option. Although the start of 2011 was not a good one, I was even more determined to further my outlook and ambition and write more so that new opportunities might open up.

All was quiet on the personal front and I wasn't that bothered either especially after the last experience!

I did four more flagship golf Caribbean cruises, one each month on *Braemar* again which certainly perked me up! Playing golf with the passengers and Harry the pro was great fun and good PR which helped as well. I would do a little set at the 19th hole (the bar!) and a fab time was had by all. There were the regular haunts and one or two surprises thrown in. I made a welcome return to Saga on the *Ruby* and the *Pearl*, working with me ole mucker Stevie Mr Banjo Galler. As before, I had to be much more laid back and slow down my delivery, they were always very appreciative and great audiences.

Like anywhere, there are some people who just don't have a sense of humour and will never laugh at anything! Old habits die hard. Is that a pun?!

My son James had been away now since September 2010 and I was looking forward to him coming home in August. The house seemed empty without him.

For some time now I had been looking after my granddaughter, Matilda, for one day each week when I was not away. She was now two years old and I loved spending time with her. She was no baby now but a very funny, gorgeous little girl.

I had enough work coming in and life was ticking away nicely but there was no sign of any romance. Maybe my chance to find the special one to spend the rest of my life with had gone.

But then, just when I thought that I had used up all my cards I was about to be dealt a winning hand and all was to change in the love stakes!

I usually like to be home on the 4th July which is my mum's birthday. My sister Jan and I take time out to celebrate this special day so I nearly didn't take the 2nd to the 9th of July Mediterranean cruise on P&O's *Ventura*.

Not really knowing why and for one reason or another I took the cruise. I have often thought that one day, somewhere down the road, or across the sea, I would meet up with a foreign lady and as luck would have it, I did. As I have already said, along came this vision from the Northern Hemisphere.

Luck or fate or being in the right place at the right time, a sequence of events brought Deborah Lesley (known by her middle name Lesley) into my world. It is said:

'Luck is what happens when fate gets tired of waiting.....'

I was lucky at last and it is also said;

'If you want something that you have never had, then you must do something you have never done.'

I had never met and socialised with a passenger before on a ship and then had any sort of relationship with one when back on land. I'm ok with an audience but one to one? With me not being much of a player or a chatter upper, this is not surprising!

I was at the bar and a girl said to me, "Do you want to dance?" I replied, "Yes." She said, "Well off you go then, I wanna get to the Bar!"

265

She said, "You look better without glasses." I said, "I'm not wearing glasses." She replied, "I know, but I am!"

I said, "I bet your face could turn a few heads" She replied, "I bet yours could turn a few stomachs!"

"What do you do for a living?" I asked. She said, "I'm a female impersonator!"

We had a date. I say date....we had a meal, watched a film, then the plane landed!

I booked a table for us one night and she wasn't happy. Apparently she didn't like snooker!

She said, "When we get married I want to share all your worries, problems and stress." I said, "I haven't got any worries, problems or stress." She replied, "You're not married yet!"

I worked the first embarkation night in the theatre on the *Ventura*. After my second sitting show I was making my way out of the side of the Theatre, carefully trying to mingle unnoticed with the passengers, when suddenly there was a tap on my shoulder.

"Excuse me, we just wanted to say how much we enjoyed your show."

I'm glad to say that many passengers compliment me after a performance, some will wait a while and others will not even bother. I find that the English can sometimes be very reserved, it can take them days to feel at ease and be friendly. This lack of confidence and reservation reminds me of a joke;

There were only two Englishmen, two Irishmen, two Scotsmen and two Welshmen on a desert island. After six months the two Scotsmen have built a distillery, the two Welshmen have formed a choir, the two Irishmen have built a road and the two Englishmen are still waiting to be introduced!

Anyway I thanked the lovely lady who was with her two grown up children and I thought that her husband was probably not too far away. Not that it made any difference to the situation.

I was wrong, he was far away, in the land of Ex! Obviously, I did not know this at the time.

The following evening I was having a quiet drink before retiring with some good friends of mine, Anna and Eamon Shepherd, the dance instructors on board, who are also from Ipswich, when along came the Angel of the North with her daughter Faye. They were walking past when I caught her eye, I called her over and gave it back to her! As she had made the effort to say hello the night before I thought I would repay the compliment, which was completely out of character for me I hasten to add. Remember I am really very shy!

She came and sat with us but there was no eye contact or any conversation between us at all so I thought no more of it.

I found out afterwards that this was because she was very nervous around me as well, so we had something in common from the word go. Thinking back, even at that very early stage there must have been some sort of attraction or spark between us.

My lovely friend Anna assured me that Lesley was on her own and that it would be a good idea for me to ask her to join us for a friendly drink.

It may sound easy. Making a girl laugh is the easy part but asking her out for a drink is the hard part! A fear of rejection came to mind! So I asked Anna to do it for me! How's that for confidence, what a wimp!

So we agreed that we would try to find Lesley the next evening. I was beginning to feel like a stalker!

My girlfriend thinks I'm a stalker. Well, she's not my girlfriend yet!

We did not have much joy to start with and just when I thought the possibility of meeting up for that friendly drink was fading, fate happened!

Anna, Eamon and myself were having dinner in the restaurant upstairs. I went to the bathroom (not to have a bath obviously!) and as I came out Lesley and I literally bumped into each other. Timing! I'm glad that I didn't go for a Scooby Doo!

She said that she had fallen asleep on her sun lounger as it was around 7.30 pm in the evening. She nervously pointed out that she wasn't looking her Sunday best and I made some pathetic comment about Worzel Gummidge and she laughed, bless her!

It didn't matter, she said she would love to go for a drink and the deed was done.

It was my mum's birthday and what a lovely present – she gave me a gift from Heaven.

Chapter Forty-One

Sofa Boy

The following day I took Lesley, Faye and Joe, her two lovely children, out for lunch in Civitavecchia. It was good, we were getting on so well, it felt natural, there were no embarrassing or awkward moments. That night, my last on the cruise, Lesley and I went for a meal together in the Italian restaurant.

Looking at the menu, she asked for the Pageoni. I said, "That is Page One!"

She wasn't feeling that good, blaming the motion of the ship. I replied, "Yes, these force one's can be a bugger!" She laughed. In fact, she laughed a lot over those last few days I had left on the ship, before I was due to fly home. The attraction was obvious and mutual and we said our goodbyes on the quayside in Livorno. As I said before, it was the first time that I had met a passenger and arranged to meet back home.

It was another two weeks before I left the following cruise at Southampton after a week on *Azura* and took the long drive up to the Northern Hemisphere. Our journey was about to begin. Manchester......fifty shades of grey! It never stops raining there!

A solid relationship needs to have solid foundations from the very start and Lesley and I have taken things slowly, albeit we lived so far apart as well.

She is an old fashioned girl in many ways, I love that about her, but she sets her standards very high, just like me! She is a great listener which is especially endearing.

She also made it very clear from the start that when I visited her in Manchester I would be sleeping on the sofa!

The guys on that *Azura* cruise ribbed me when I told them this in the Temple Bar in Dublin and consequently christened me...... Sofa Boy! It sounds like a lazy Superhero!

Since meeting Lesley, work has continued to flourish but I have been keeping the cruising dates to suit us somewhat. From our first *Ventura* cruise up until the end of this book we have been on many cruises together and visited some fantastic places.

The one-nighters and the free weekends meant that we have been able to see each other most of the time. All in all we have made the date sheet work for us.

'Work to live, not live to work'.

Shorter cruises have become more practical in helping us avoid spending too much time apart. I have found out the hard way that for a relationship to develop and last you have to spend most of the time together!

The future now looks very bright for us as Lesley has just completed her fifth and final year of Counselling training and moved down South as being apart is not an option for us.

Five months into our relationship Lesley's mum passed away. I had the good fortune of meeting Pat on a few occasions and she was a great lady and very much in the mould of my dear mum.

It is strange how life pans out. Lesley had just driven down south to me as we had arranged to celebrate my birthday with a few close friends. No sooner had she arrived then the dreaded phone call came and we immediately drove back to Manchester.

It was a very sad and traumatic time, Lesley had cared for her mum for quite a while and I was so glad to be with her in her time of grief.

We often talk of our dear mums and dads as Lesley had lost her dear dad the year before. We laugh and cry together and count our blessings and we are very thankful that they all lived to a ripe old age.

After just over a year together I got down on one knee and proposed to Lesley. Without hesitation she helped me up and said, "Yes".

Our plans to wed are very much on the horizon and we both cannot wait to be together. We don't like the North South divide.

John Booth, a great friend of mine had been my best man at two of my previous weddings. I said to him, I hope you don't mind if I don't ask you this time John. You're a bloody jinx mate......only joking!

It was now the time that Toby James came into the world, my first grandson. Wow! Claire encountered a few problems to begin with but all has turned out well. He is a gorgeous, blue eyed blonde and he is already walking and talking. He'll be tweeting before you know it!

Matilda is now five, going on fifteen! She got an I-pad for her birthday. When I was five I was lucky to get a writing pad!

"Do you want to write a letter to Santa to ask him what you want him to bring you for Christmas?" She said, "No pops, I'm going to send him a text!" How times have changed.

Her uncle James is living in Hanoi, Vietnam at the moment and she only sees him on the computer using wi -fi. I asked her: "Do you know where your uncle James lives?" She replied, "He lives in Skype!".....

To cap it all James came home to see his newborn nephew and it was great to see him.

The last three years have been fruitful to say the least especially with my lady inspiring me on. She loves comedy and loves to laugh. Can you imagine being with someone who has no sense of humour – oh yes, the ex wife!

I have never been too keen on fly backs (flying out to do shows in hotels abroad) but a two nighter for Thomson Gold Hotels in Ibiza came up and it was great fun working outside by the pool.

There are now many cruise companies with their own liners and it is always a refreshing change to add a new ship to the mix. The *Celebrity Eclipse*, P&O's *Adonia* with one of my best mates and a wonderful variety act Leo Shavers, and the *Crown Princess* to mention a few. My good friend Jo Martin looks after me when it comes to the American ships and I hope there will be lots more of these in the future. It is so important to keep that healthy balance between being at home and being away. Short haul and short cruises are top of the pecking order.

I did a handful of short cruises on *Crown Princess* and it was good to work with a fab singer of Les Miserable fame, Nik Page, and some other talented funny guys; David Copperfield, Marc Walker, Philip Hitchcock, and my mates of old, Gary T Thompson and Jimmy the Vent Tamley. Jimmy and I go back a long way, he's got more kids than puppets. Slow down Jim!

The *Oceana* came calling once again, it had been a few years, and it was made extra special because my mate Paul Emmanuel was on as well. We hadn't worked together for a few years and it was quite a while since we had been on this ship. He is star quality just like so many others I have had the pleasure of sharing the same stage with. Only a few weeks ago I worked alongside Steve Larkins, a fantastic Freddie Mercury tribute and a great character. What a great business show-business is, you meet some amazingly talented people and with some you make lifelong friendships and that makes it even more rewarding. With others, it's like ships in the night, you meet them once and never see them again.

A few of the artists on ships are celebs and household names, but most of us are not. It doesn't matter.

It is so satisfying to be able to work with nice friends and have some sort of camaraderie especially recently with Roy and Sonia, aka Melody Lane, a fab double act in more ways than one! Fred Olsen also has many talented performers on their ships and it's a bonus when you can work with other great comedy acts, the likes of Bob Webb, Taffy Spencer and Dave Bonnie Lad Kristian.

Potters at Hopton, near Great Yarmouth, has and still is a regular venue for me. It is a fab place to work, quite exclusive and my shows there are always so well received. I look forward to performing in their wonderful theatre whether it be a midweek bowls audience, the Friday late nights or a Sunday lunchtime.

From the man himself, John Potter, to Nigel and Rachel the bookers, and Mark, Busby, Richard, Johnny and all the gang, it is a pleasure to be part of the set-up there.

I enjoyed a Variety Club stag luncheon in Jersey for my buddy Paul Wagner, then topped the bill at the annual Max Miller Appreciation Society in Brighton working once again with the very talented ventriloquist Steve Hewlett. I then did a night with Puppetry of the Penis at the Hexagon Theatre in Reading for Trish and Nick, from NETT UK which kept me well and truly on my toes (I hasten to add that I was supporting and not doing any of the puppetry!) It's not often you get the chance, thank goodness, to support two naked men doing various things with their genitalia! I don't mean physically either!

After a short cruise on *Arcadia*, I flew from Constanza, Romania to Istanbul with their local airline, Carpet Air. A few weeks later I flew from Robin Hood Airport near Doncaster, to Gydnia in Poland with Wizzair. I couldn't make this up, people wouldn't believe me!

The Carpet Air flight was an interesting experience to say the least, the plane was a very small propeller job! When I arrived at the airport, I say airport loosely, there were no planes or passengers anywhere to be seen. After two hours a plane turned up and four of us got on!

I asked the man at check-in, "Can I have a window seat?" He replied, "They are all window seats!"

He gave me Seat 2A and I said, "Can I sit near the back?" He replied, "2A is at the back!"

271

The flight attendants were no spring chickens! They had certainly been around the eastern block a few times. I know, clever, but funny!

So without taking on too much and with my fiancée in sunny Manchester a very healthy balance between work and play has been my target.

Learn from yesterday and live for today.

The past is history, the future is a mystery, today is a gift, and that's why they call it the present'.

2013 was a very eventful year for me and Lesley. We had a Caribbean cruise on *Ventura*, then a five day holiday in New York where we had an absolutely fantastic time. Neither of us had been there before and we took in all the sights and we never wasted a second.

There were three Canary Island cruises on *Braemar* including a two week Easter cruise with Lesley. The summer was busy and the best weather-wise for some time.

My great friend Steve Hewlett, the ventriloquist, asked me to join him with a few other guys to go to BBC Scotland in Glasgow and record the popular BBC quiz programme Eggheads, a celebrity episode. Our team name was Stevie's Dummies and we had a fun day out and came away with our heads held high. We came second!

It made a nice change to be back on TV, albeit with no audience.

It was even more special this year to do a Fred Olsen cruise in aid of the Bobby Robson Cancer Fund. Several thousand pounds were raised and a few of the Ipswich Town ex-players were on that three day cruise, George Burley, Brian Hamilton and Allan Hunter. The *Black Watch* sailed from Harwich to Newcastle, two clubs that Sir Bobby managed with great success. Sharing the bill was my buddy Dave Kristian. Ipswich v Newcastle, we drew 1 – 1 (won, won)!

This is such a fitting end as I sit here and reminisce about all those years ago when my hero Sir Bobby won the FA Cup with my home club Ipswich, and I had just started my journey into comedy that very same day. I remember those times with great affection.

2012 Braemar with
Taffy, Jamie, Paul & Ian

The girls at Fred Olsen, Ipswich;
Anna, Louise, Helen and Barbara

Crown Princess 2013 with
Nik Page & Gary T. Thompson

Crown Princess 2013
with ventriliquoist Jimmy Tamley

January 2013 on top
of the Empire State
Building New York
with Lesley

Bobby Robson Cancer Charity
on Black Watch June 2013 with
Richard, Judy, Derek, Linda
and Lesley

Me and Lesley
crusing in 2013

274

2013 November, on Braemar with Des O'Connor

December 2013 with Berys & the gang from P&O at Carnival House in Southampton

September 2014 on Oceana
with world famous Astro Physicist, Professor Stephen Hawking

My Stag Night, August 2014, with the lads from Rushmere Golf Club, The party and golf was at 'Langdon Hills' golf Club near Basildon, Thanks Johnny.

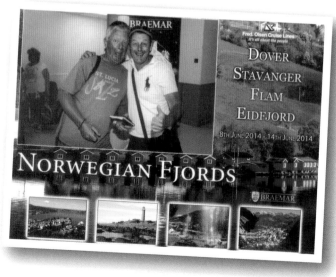

Messing around with my 'Best Man' Leo Shavers at Dover Terminal

The Wedding, August 2014

The family photo which appeared in 'Hello' magazine!
Faye, Joe, Lesley, Claire, Toby, myself and Matilda

My Angel
of the North,
Lesley

Toby & Matilda in their den!

Me, Claire & James, Christmas 2014

In memory of my Mum & Dad xx

Chapter Forty-Two

Rock My World Funny Boy!

The year 2013 ended with an opera cruise with Kathryn Jenkins on *Oriana* and performing alongside Des O'Connor on the *Braemar* and Michael Ball on *Aurora*. On New Year's Eve Lesley and I were on *Aurora* once again to see the amazing fireworks extravaganza in Madeira. Wow! It is also Lesley's birthday on New Year's Eve and it was certainly a night to remember. A memorable cruise to say the least.

At the start of 2014 I was on Saga *Sapphire* and who should I bump into.... Murray Walker! We reminisced about that night on *Arcadia* when we had the Formula One Scalextric race. It was lovely to see him again, he didn't look a day over ninety!

Having celebrated over twenty-five years cruising with P&O, the future still looks bright on the horizon. I was first given the chance by the then booker, David Llewellyn, back in 1989. Then Anthony Radford took the helm followed by Peter Allen and now I am dealing with the wonderful Berys Said who I have known for many years. She oversees all the guys and girls in the head office in Southampton who look after me very well. To me, respect is everything and I often call in to see them for a chat. I have come a long way since those early days on *Canberra*, not only in experience but all those miles as well. I often wonder how many miles I have travelled. I wish I could have collected sea miles!

Let your memory be your travel bag....

It has been so satisfying writing this book and I am glad that it has taken so long for many reasons.

Since the idea first came to write this adventure over ten years ago, so much has happened. In my personal life alone I have had two divorces, lost my wonderful mum and dad and had a cancer scare. My beautiful daughter Claire has given me two gorgeous grandchildren and I have met the love of my life, my soul mate Lesley.

My son James, who I am so proud of, has been away for a while now working in Hanoi, Vietnam. He enjoys his work and life there and is very happy. That is all you want for your kids at the end of the day, for them to be happy and enjoy life. I do not tell him but I think he knows that I wish he was here at home. Lesley and I have just been out there to see him for a week. It was so good to see where he works and lives. Vietnam is such a wonderful, vibrant place. There are eight million people in Hanoi and five million scooters!

I miss him so much.

As you have read, I have met many special people over the years and having recently been on *Oceana*, who should be on there but the world famous Astro Physicist Professor Stephen Hawking. He came to my show with his nurses and carers and in his own way said how much he enjoyed my performance. What a remarkable man and it was a real honour to meet him. A moment to savour.

I have overlooked, glossed over and probably forgotten all the hundreds and hundreds of the greatly satisfying and successful gigs I have done throughout my career and concentrated on the more obscure, difficult and interesting ones.

I end this story at a point where it is nearly thirty-seven years since I first walked onto a stage on my own and made people laugh. I had no act whatsoever then and it has certainly been an adventure. I am amazed that I have remembered so much and glad that I kept some notes and records along the way.

There are probably many other interesting and funny stories and events that I have forgotten but most importantly to all the wonderful characters I have met and worked with but not mentioned..... I apologise profusely.

What this life as a comedian has given me is the joy of meeting and performing with so many talented and special people.

I miss them and hope to meet up with them again someday.

When two people become best friends, great lovers and then soul mates, they become one. Lesley and I are totally in love with each other and cannot bear to be apart. I have waited a long time to feel this way.

I have now found the love of my life who has given me so many feelings and emotions. She makes me feel wanted in every way. I feel like standing on the tallest building and telling the whole world I am alive again and finally have met someone who gets me!

In fact, I did this on our trip to New York. I shouted this from the hundred and second floor of the Empire State Building!!

I have met someone who wants to get inside my head and my heart. She has made me complete and I know we are perfect for each other in every way.

Lesley is my safe place to fall and vice versa......I look forward to loving her more and more each day.

We have both experienced loss, hurt and sadness along the way but I believe that's what gives us our depth and character and togetherness in all the things we do.

In life it is rare to find someone that you can connect with on every level...... sometimes timing is everything! I know that fate brought us together and luck played its part as well.

To the world you are one person. To one person you are the world......

Even though I still love what I do with a great passion, I feel that I am at a time in my life where being a comedian and making people laugh for a living isn't the be all and end all.

I am very fortunate to have found someone who actually loves what I do and all that goes with it. Lesley absolutely adores cruising which is an extra bonus and will be a big plus for us over the coming years.

The world is a book and those who do not travel read only one page......

It has taken many years for me to find my special one and I am now in a very happy place. I enjoy going to work and have met my Angel of the North to share my life with.

As my story so far is coming to an end what a better way to celebrate it than my wedding to Lesley.

We had such a fantastic day at the Orwell Hotel in Felixstowe, where I have had many a great time with my very good friend, the entrepreneur, Richard

Cattermole. No expense was spared and Lesley's hard work in organizing the whole event to the last detail really stole the show. It was an emotional ceremony and a wonderful occasion with all our friends and family there to share it with us. Claire gave a perfect reading from Captain Correlli's Mandolin, Matilda was a flower girl and Toby a page boy, them being there was the icing on the cake. Lesley's son Joe walked her down the aisle and gave her away and Faye was maid of honour with Lesley's niece Megan as bridesmaid. It really was a family affair! Lots of Lesley's family and friends came down from Manchester to celebrate our special day with us. Our wedding photograph appeared in the 22nd December 2014 issue of Hello magazine........we are still waiting for the one hundred thousand pounds appearance fee!!

Afterwards we jetted off to Venice for three days, staying at the Rialto Hotel right in the centre of the city just by the Rialto Bridge. We took in a gondola ride around the canals (I sang Just One Cornetto!), we visited the Basilica in St. Mark's Square and had a night at the opera.

On the final morning we were taken by speedboat from our hotel around the canals, out on to the open waters and direct to the P&O *Ventura's* berth. We sailed for a week around Italy from Venice to Livorno and had such a fabulous honeymoon, the *Ventura* was where it all began for us just over three years earlier.

I wrote this next piece whilst waiting for a laugh once. I'd read the book and then the film came out, so I put pen to paper, and this is it:

It was their Golden Wedding
  She went to bed at 8
He stayed up to watch the football
  She whispered 'Don't be Late'

The wife, she had this book
  She'd been reading it all day
What he didn't know
  It was 50 Shades of Grey

When he walked into the bedroom
  She slowly began to strip
In one hand she had some rope
  In the other she had a whip

Now 50 years ago
  He would have been at his peak
His body's not the same no more
  He's 86 next week

She handed him the rope
  And said: 'Tie me to the bed'
In a sexy voice: 'Do what you like'
  He went down the pub instead

He came back with some bravado
  Explored her body for a while
He tried in vain but yet again
  couldn't even raise a smile

No matter what she did
  She couldn't turn him on
His nights between the sheets
  were well and truly gone

She saw his naked body
  And put the toys away
The man she met all those years ago
  Had turned 50 Shades of Grey.

Chapter Forty-Three

Encore

Comedy has many extremes. You can play very safe sometimes and go well over the top the next.

It is an art form, a craft, and you need to make it look natural and unscripted, not making it seem like you've done it a million times before and are just going through the motions. You have to gauge your audience quickly. On some occasions you need to hold back but ideally for me it is more fun to go right to the line – but never cross it.

Comedy material can be described as either an objective look at reality or a biased look at reality, depending on the content of the joke. However, it is all based on realism and how we look at life and our concept of it.

Shoot for the moon and even if you miss, you will land amongst the stars.

The shortest distance between two people is a smile and a smile is the same in every language.

You don't stop laughing when you grow old, you grow old when you stop laughing.

There are no secrets to success. It is a result of preparation, hard work and learning from failure.

Take chances and have no fear – the only thing to fear is fear itself.

Why does the butterfly fly outside the box?
I fly outside the box because I can.
But we know the box, we are safe inside the box.
That is why I leave it,
For you may be safe, but I am free!

I hope that I will have everlasting happiness with my new love.
I hope that my children and their children will live long and happy lives.
I hope that I will make people laugh for many more years to come.

Live life
Love unconditionally
Laugh uncontrollably

Acknowledgments

I would like to thank the following people who have helped me make this book possible.

John McNally for his proof reading skills and Leo Shavers, Steve Stone and all at ColourplanPrint for their assistance with the printing.

My Lesley for typing the manuscript from my scrawling notes and completing the final editing.....it certainly was a labour of love!

And finally, to all my family and friends who have helped me along the way......I thank you.

"After nearly three decades involved with entertainment at Potters Leisure Resort I have seen many fine comics, but only a select few allow me to relax knowing they will constantly deliver. Micky is the top of that list. Always evolving, always writing he never fails to judge his audience correctly and give them exactly what they want. Without doubt one of the finest comics working today."
Nigel Pattle - Entertainments Creative Director - Potters at Hopton

"Micky is the 'go to' comic that you can book with confidence. He has the ability to entertain every audience whether they are young or simply young at heart!"
Berys Said - Entertainment Booking and Programme Manager Carnival UK

"Micky is now performing on RCCL, Princess and Celebrity cruise lines with great success, a comedy entertainer of the highest quality. He cleverly adapts his style and material to suit the American audiences as well......he makes people laugh!"
Joanne Martin - Jo Martin Management

"Micky is one of our top entertainers, he constantly introduces new material which is current and topical. He is a firm favourite with our guests."
Helen Bennett - Entertainments Manager - Fred Olsen Cruise Lines

"Micky is a true professional with a natural flair for comedy. I haven't seen one audience that has not loved, laughed and applauded his individual style and talent, a pleasure to work with and a joy to have on board."
Andy Mills-Brown - Senior Cruise Director - Fred Olsen Cruise Lines

"A wonderful evening: Micky cleverly adapted his act from what could have been a difficult situation with ladies present, but he brought the house down, more important he kept it clean."
Mary Nicklen - Chief Executive - Children Say Charity

"For the past ten years since he first started cruising on the Saga Rose world cruise in 2003, Micky has been a breath of fresh air for our more mature passengers. His comedy presentation and content is of the highest quality and he achieves excellent ratings with our passengers.....he delivers every time."
Joanne Lister-Ward - Leisure Services Manager - SAGA Cruises